Salvation Sermons

by
Oliver B. Greene

The Gospel Hour, Inc., Oliver B. Greene, Director
Box 2024, Greenville, South Carolina 29602

First printing, July 1970—15,000 copies
Second printing, October 1970—15,000 copies
Third printing, January 1973—15,000 copies
Fourth printing, February 1974—15,000 copies
Fifth printing, November 1974—15,000 copies
Sixth printing, May 1976—15,000 copies

$5.00

FOREWORD

There is much need for pure Bible teaching today, that God's children may grow in grace and in the knowledge of the things of God. But with the unrest and turmoil that embraces the world, there is also a need for the message of salvation. People are seeking peace and rest, but the only peace and rest on earth today is in the hearts of God's people. There is neither peace *nor* rest outside of Christ.

This book is sent out with the sincere prayer that through the salvation messages it contains, hearts may find rest because souls find Christ in forgiveness of sins.

—The Author

Contents

Contents

WHY JESUS CHRIST
CAME INTO THE WORLD

Why Jesus Christ
Came Into the World

"This is a faithful saying, and worthy of all acceptance, that *Christ Jesus came into the world to save sinners . . ."* (I Tim. 1:15).

The subject of this message has engaged the thoughtful and earnest attention of theologians, historians, political philosophers, reformers, and religionists for many, many years.

There are those who tell us that Christ came into the world to set an example, and that men should *follow* His example.

Others tell us that He came to proclaim the fatherhood of God and the brotherhood of man.

Still others declare that He came into the world to carry to completion God's original thought in the creation of man.

Some say that Christ came into the world to reorganize society and clean up the world, to establish a form of human government which would be *righteous* in its rule, a government through which He would bring the kingdom of God to this earth.

There are some who tell us that He came to teach and to heal.

9

Many and varied are the ideas and philosophies as to why Jesus Christ came into the world; but the real answer is found in the one short verse of Scripture used as our text. It is not *man's* answer, it is *God's* answer given to Paul through the Holy Spirit and penned down for our instruction and admonition. As Paul explained to young Timothy:

"ALL Scripture is given by inspiration of God, and is profitable for doctrine, for reproof, for correction, for instruction in righteousness: that the man of God may be perfect, throughly furnished unto all good works"* (II Tim. 3:16, 17).

Peter also explains "that no prophecy of the Scripture is of any private interpretation. For the prophecy came not in old time by the will of man: but holy men of God spake as they were moved by the Holy Ghost" (II Pet. 1:20, 21).

No Need to Speculate

There is no need to speculate as to why the Lord Jesus Christ came into the world, for God Himself has clearly *revealed* why He came:

"This is a faithful saying . . . ." That is, the words we are reading are trustworthy, we need not hesitate or fear to believe them.

". . . and worthy of all acceptation . . . ." This *"faithful* saying" is also *"worthy,"* deserving of our complete acceptance.

". . . Christ Jesus came into the world to save

10

sinners." This is the faithful, worthy saying—the answer to why the Lord Jesus Christ came into the world: He came *to save sinners.*

Many times throughout the Gospels and the epistles we find this same truth stated in different words. For example, in Matthew 20:28 we read:

"Even as the Son of man came not to be ministered unto, but to minister, and *to give His life a ransom for many."*

Luke 19:10 tells us, "The Son of man is come *to seek and to save that which was lost."*

Yes, the meaning of this faithful, worthy saying is clear: "Christ Jesus came into the world *to save sinners."* Read those words—and re-read them. Reflect upon their exact meaning and tremendous force. To me, the words of our text are incredible words, for they unmistakably declare that it was in the interest of depraved, hell-deserving sinners— vile, wretched outcasts, rebels against God—that the glorious Son of God left heaven's glory and in a body of humiliation came to earth to tabernacle among men. Not for the *righteous,* but for thieves, robbers, harlots, bandits, murderers, God's Christ came down in a body of flesh—and He came full of saving grace and full of truth:

"The Word was made flesh, and dwelt among us, (and we beheld His glory, the glory as of the only begotten of the Father,) full of grace and truth" (John 1:14). Jesus declared, "Ye shall know the *truth,* and the truth shall make you free"

11

(John 8:32).

Christ Jesus came into the world to *save* sinners, not to condemn them to an eternity in hell. It has been said that ministers enjoy preaching "hell-fire and damnation," but this is not true. God's man *must* preach that there is a hell and that the wrath of God is poured out upon the ungodly; but he also finds great joy in telling men that Christ died for our sins according to the Scriptures, and that it is not God's will that any be lost but that all repent and be saved. Jesus did not come into the world to destroy the world, but that the world through Him—but mind you, *ONLY through Him*—might be saved.

"For God so LOVED the world, that He gave His only begotten Son, that whosoever believeth in Him should not perish, but have everlasting life. For God sent not His Son into the world to *CONDEMN the world,* but that the world through Him *might be SAVED"* (John 3:16, 17).

Yes, as *man* thinks, it is incredible that God's only Son should leave the Father's bosom, step down from His throne, lay aside His infinite glory, and consent to take a body of humiliation that He might enter this world through the womb of a virgin. And from the day He was wrapped in swaddling clothes and laid in a manger His eye was singled on the dreadful cross of Golgotha. All of this He did in order to save wretched, miserable, hell-deserving sinners. Is it not incredible?

No wonder the Apostle Paul, inspired of the Holy Ghost, found it necessary to preface his declaration with the statement that what he was saying was "a *faithful* saying, and *worthy of all acceptation.*" Paul knew philosophers and their way of thinking. He knew they would not accept such a statement as being reasonable answer to why Christ came into the world. Therefore he called attention to the fact that unbelievable as the statement seemed to be, the words were—and are—*true.* They are God's own words, words worthy of man's unquestioning and absolute confidence and acceptance.

It was not on behalf of those who love and worship Him that Christ came into the world. He came on behalf of those who do not love and worship Him. He came on behalf of sinners—a word seldom used in the modern pulpit, *never* used in the pulpits of liberals and modernists. Men do not like to be called sinners—in fact, very few people will admit that they *are* sinners. The most difficult thing confronting God's minister today is the task of getting unsaved people to see their lost condition and their need of a Saviour. No one will call on God for mercy and salvation until he first recognizes that he is a sinner.

In Romans 3:9-12 the Apostle Paul declares that *all* are under sin—"As it is written, There is none righteous, no, not one. There is none that understandeth, there is none that seeketh after God.

They are all gone out of the way, they are together become unprofitable; there is none that doeth good, no, not one." Then in verse 23 of that same chapter he declares, *"For ALL have sinned, and come short of the glory of God!"*

Sin is the most loathsome, hateful thing in all the universe! All disease, corruption, rottenness, death—everything disgusting and repulsive—is because of sin. (Now I did not say that all *sinners* are loathsome and hateful, or repulsive and disgusting. I said *sin* is all of those things—and much, much more.) However, the sinner is *capable* (and some are guilty) of *the personal embodiment* of all things vile and repulsive. But the Lord Jesus Christ came into this world to die for sinners, regardless of the depth of sin to which the sinner has gone.

In Mark 7:21-23 Jesus describes the capability of the heart of a sinner:

"From within, out of the heart of men, proceed evil thoughts, adulteries, fornications, murders, thefts, covetousness, wickedness, deceit, lasciviousness, an evil eye, blasphemy, pride, foolishness. All these evil things come *from within,* and defile the man!" A person who is not a born again child of God is capable of committing any or all of the sins named in these verses from the Gospel of Mark.

The Apostle Paul testified, "We ourselves also were sometimes foolish, disobedient, deceived, serving divers lusts and pleasures, living in malice and envy, hateful, and hating one another" (Tit. 3:3).

Again—I am not saying that all sinners think dirty thoughts, commit adultery, murder, steal, live a wicked life of deceit and blasphemy. But I do say that any man or woman who is not born again has within his or her bosom a heart capable of finding out any sin that has ever been committed by mortal man, no matter how hideous that sin may be! Yet—regardless of how ungodly and wicked the sinner, Jesus is seeking to save that sinner. While He tabernacled among men here on earth, those people with whom He met most often were men and women who were sinners.

His enemies said of Him, "This Man receiveth sinners, and eateth with them" (Luke 15:2). His own people, the Jews, criticized Him for eating "with publicans and sinners" (Matt. 9:11). They called Him a "winebibber, a friend of publicans and sinners" (Matt. 11:19). Jesus Himself boldly declared, "I came not to call the righteous, but sinners to repentance" (Mark 2:17).

He who came into the world to save sinners dealt kindly and lovingly with those who came to Him for salvation. To Nicodemus He simply explained, "Ye must be born again. . . . Marvel not that I said unto thee, Ye must be born again." (Read John 3:3-7.) Nicodemus was a very prominent, respected, religious Jew, a teacher in Israel, and he knew the Old Testament prophecies concerning the coming of the Lamb of God and the reason for His coming. He was a sincere seeker of truth, and Jesus answered him in few words. There was no need to go into detail with Nicodemus as He did with some of the other sinners with whom He dealt.

With the fallen woman of Samaria who came to Jacob's well to draw water while Jesus rested there, He discussed many things—the living water, the true way of worship, His own messianic office. When at last she said, "Sir, give me this water" Jesus replied, "Go, call thy husband, and come hither." Thus did He reveal to her that even though He had never met her previously, He knew her past and her present life. Step by step He led her to the door of salvation, and when He said to her, "I that speak unto thee am (Messiah)" she was ready to receive the truth. Those seven words brought faith to her heart, and she ran into the city to tell the men that she had found the Christ. Read John 4:1-29.

In Luke 19:1-10 we read of Zacchaeus, a wealthy tax collector, "chief among the publicans." Being small of stature, Zacchaeus climbed up in a sycamore tree in order to see over the heads of the crowd as Jesus passed by. He longed for a look at Jesus, but no doubt he was surprised when the Lord looked up, saw him in the sycamore tree, and said to him: "Zacchaeus, make haste, and come down; for to day I must abide at thy house." He hastened down from the tree, received Jesus joyfully, and in verses 9 and 10 of that passage Jesus declared to him:

"This day is salvation come to this house . . . for the Son of man is come to seek and to save that which was lost!"

Any man with a sincere desire to see Jesus *will see Him* because Jesus is still seeking sinners. He is seeking *you* if you are not saved. He is seeking you *now,* through this message.

We might look at one more instance where a poor, lost sinner came to Jesus. It was in the home of Simon the Pharisee that Jesus sat at meat that day. "And, behold, a woman in the city, which was a sinner, when she knew that Jesus sat at meat in the Pharisee's house, brought an alabaster box of ointment, and stood at His feet behind Him weeping, and began to wash His feet with tears, and did wipe them with the hairs of her head, and kissed His feet, and anointed them with the ointment."

When Simon saw this he said "within himself," "If this Man were really a prophet He would not allow this woman to touch Him, for she is a sinner." Jesus in His omniscience discerned Simon's thoughts and said to him, "There was a certain creditor which had two debtors. The one owed five hundred pence, the other fifty. Neither of them had money to pay, and the creditor forgave

17

them both. Tell me—which of them will love him most?" Simon of course replied, "I suppose he to whom he forgave most." Jesus said, "Thou hast rightly judged."

Then of the woman He said, "Her sins, which are many, are forgiven; for she loved much: but to whom little is forgiven, the same loveth little." To the woman He said, *"Thy sins are forgiven. . . . Thy FAITH hath saved thee.* Go in peace" (Luke 7:36-50).

Please notice this woman was saved in the one and only way of salvation. Jesus said, *"Thy FAITH hath saved thee."* There is only one way to get faith—"faith cometh by hearing, and hearing by the Word of God" (Rom. 10:17). I would emphasize that this woman had heard the words of Jesus —probably standing in the shadows while He preached in the streets of the city. She believed His words, she went to the house of Simon the Pharisee while Jesus was visiting there, and she fell at His feet in humble, complete submission. Her tears were tears of repentance. She had faith, her faith brought her to Jesus, and He saved her.

He is still seeking sinners—thieves, harlots, drunkards—yea, and pious religious church members! He is still tender and kind toward sinners. He graciously invites, "Come unto me, and I will give you rest. Come unto me, I will in no wise cast you out!"

Yes, Jesus was gracious to sinners, kind and

gentle as He invited them to come to Him; but He was merciless to the religionists and moralists who boasted of their own righteousness! He saw through their profession. He stripped away their veneer of morality and decency, their superficial covering of religious forms, long prayers, embroidered garments, and exposed the iniquity and ungodliness within their hearts. He pronounced "Woe!" upon them, denouncing them as "hypocrites . . . blind guides . . . fools . . . ." He likened them to "whited sepulchres, which indeed appear beautiful outward, but are within full of dead men's bones, and of all uncleanness." He declared, "Ye also outwardly appear righteous unto men, but within ye are full of hypocrisy and iniquity." He called them "serpents . . . generation of vipers," and asked, "How can ye escape the damnation of hell?" (Matt. 23:13-33).

Time and space will not permit me to quote the entire chapter here, but if you will read Matthew chapter 23 you will read one of the most scorching messages ever to fall from the lips of man. But from the same lips fell the tenderest, most compassionate words ever spoken by man, words in the interest of poor, wretched sinners! Thus are we reminded that God is love (I John 4:8), but He is also a consuming fire (Heb. 12:29).

Are You Saved?

Today when people are asked "Would you like

to be saved?" the answer usually is "I am a church member." Or "I was christened (confirmed or baptized) when I was a baby." Or "I joined the church in my youth, I have been a church member for many years." Or "I live a good life, I do the best I can. I live by the Golden Rule." A person who answers in this manner is almost always lost. "Religious"? Yes—but lost. Morally upright and honest? Perhaps—but lost. And it is absolutely essential that a person *admit* to being lost before he can be saved.

The Apostle Paul said, "I am chief of sinners." Yet if you were to study the history of his life you would find that he lived after the straitest sect of the Pharisees. He was devoted to the religion of his fathers. True, he consented to the death of Stephen—but he thought he was doing God a favor. He arrested and imprisoned Christians—but he thought Christians were enemies of God. However, on the Damascus road, the moment Saul of Tarsus realized who Jesus was, he turned from the religion of Judaism to the Lord Jesus Christ and was saved. Please study Acts chapter 9.

Beloved, if *you* are saved, you are saved because sometime, somewhere, in your past life you recognized your lost condition and came to Jesus! You confessed that you were a poor, lost sinner, and you received Him by faith as your own personal Saviour.

If you cannot remember such an experience, you are still lost! I do not say that you must remember the time of day, the day of the week, the date, the month, or even the year. But if you cannot remember a time when you realized that you were hopelessly lost and on the road to hell, and called on Jesus for the forgiveness of your sins, then I declare without fear or apology *you had better have such an experience,* or you will spend eternity in hell. My dear church member, morally clean lady or gentleman, have *you* approached God as a sinner, pleading the blood of Jesus for the remission of sins? If you have not, then bear in mind that Jesus came into the world to save sinners, and He cannot save you until you recognize the fact that you *are* a sinner, and are willing to accept His salvation.

Denominational churches today are filled with people who are strictly "religious" on Sunday, and then they forget God until the *next* Sunday. Of such Jesus declared, "Verily I say unto you, That the publicans and the harlots go into the kingdom of God before you" (Matt. 21:31). That does not mean that publicans and harlots will go into heaven apart from redemption. No indeed! It simply means that publicans and harlots will recognize their lost condition while many church people do not see their own need of a Saviour.

I repeat—people do not like to be referred to as "sinners." They do not like to face the solemn fact that they are hell-deserving because of their sin. But unless one comes to Jesus as a lost sinner, that one will never step inside the gates of that beautiful city. To His own people, the Jews, Jesus said, "Search the Scriptures; for in them ye think ye have eternal life: and they are they which testify of me. *And YE WILL NOT come to me*, that ye might have life" (John 5:39, 40).

John 18:28 tells us that when the Jews finally demanded that Jesus be crucified and He was arrested and taken before Pilate, *"they themselves went not into the judgment hall, lest they should be defiled; but that they might eat the Passover."* These people were so "religious" they would not go into the judgment hall because they wanted to observe the Passover, and if they entered the judgment hall they would be ceremonially defiled and could not carry out the religious ceremony. But their religion blinded them to the fact that they were demanding the death of the One who had come to save them.

In our local churches today there are people who are so busy with their religious activities that they do not have time to get saved! They are so busy keeping the denominational machinery running, attending meetings, serving on committees, carrying out the "program" of the denomination, that they have not time to recognize their lost condition. Religious? Definitely so!

But sadly lost.

Bible Comparisons

In the Bible, sinners are compared to many things. I cannot give the text of all these comparisons here, but please read each of the Scripture references I am giving. The Word of God compares the sinner to the following:

The uncleanliness of the dog (Prov. 26:11).

The stubbornness of the donkey (Job 11:12).

The subtlety of the snake (Matt. 23:33).

The devouring wolf (John 10:12).

The wild boar (Psalm 80:13).

The wallowing of the hog in the mire (II Pet. 2:22).

The cruelty of the bear (Prov. 28:15).

The fox (Luke 13:32).

The poison of the viper (Matt. 23:33).

The stupidity of the sheep (Isa. 53:6).

The ravening of the lion (Psalm 22:13).

Under inspiration of the Holy Spirit, the Apostle Paul penned the following word-picture of sinners:

"Their throat is an open sepulchre; with their tongues they have used deceit; the poison of asps is under their lips:` whose mouth is full of cursing and bitterness. Their feet are swift to shed blood. Destruction and misery are in their ways: and the way of peace have they not known. There is no fear of God before their eyes" (Rom. 3:13-18).

I am not saying that all unbelievers fit these

comparisons. I am simply saying that *the Word of God* makes such comparisons, and certainly a sinner *even at his best* is unfit for the kingdom of God! Anyone who hopes to enter heaven must be born from above, created anew in Christ Jesus through the miracle of His shed blood. Anyone rejecting the blood of Jesus and the cleansing power of His blood cannot enter the kingdom of heaven. You need not, like Paul, confess to being *chief* of sinners; but it is divinely imperative that you face the fact that you *are* a sinner—and until you face that fact, God cannot and will not save your soul!

What Was the Purpose of Christ Jesus Concerning Sinners?

It was on behalf of sinners that the Lord Jesus Christ left the Father's bosom, took a body of humiliation, and in that body came into the world; but what was *His purpose concerning sinners?* He came into the world on their behalf, but what did He come to do for them? Our text answers: *He came to SAVE them.*

The purpose of Christ concerning sinners was not to condemn them to hell. He did not come to upbraid them and run them down in words of scorn. He did not come to reform them and make them better citizens. He did not come to help them live better lives. *He came to SAVE*—freely, fully, and forever! Nothing can be added to the salvation God provided through Jesus Christ our Saviour. God is perfect and we are saved with a perfect salvation—the gift of God. When Jesus saves, He saves perfectly and eternally. He gives the believing sinner eternal life.

There is much ignorance, even among born again people, concerning salvation and what it means to be saved. Many people are saved and in the Church, they know they are saved and that their salvation delivers them from the fires of hell— and they are satisfied to stop there. But salvation consists of much more than deliverance from the torments of an eternal hell.

God is holy, and because of God's holiness, *sin* separates man from God. The wrath of God is kindled against the sinner, and that wrath can be removed only by and through the finished work of the Lord Jesus Christ. "He that believeth on the Son hath everlasting life: and he that believeth not the Son shall not see life; but the wrath of God abideth on him" (John 3:36). But even though the wrath of God is kindled against the sinner, God loves the sinner; and the Lord Jesus Christ came into the world to save sinners from the guilt of sin, to save from the wrath of God which abides on the sinner, and to give peace within:

"Therefore being justified by faith, we have peace with God through our Lord Jesus Christ: by whom also we have access by faith into this grace wherein we stand, and rejoice in hope of the glory of God" (Rom. 5:1, 2). Jesus said to His disciples, "Peace I leave with you, *MY peace* I give unto you. Not as the world giveth, give I unto you. Let not your heart be troubled, neither let it be afraid" (John 14:27).

How does Christ Jesus save sinners from their guilt and remove that guilt from our conscience? The answer is found in Galatians 3:13:

"Christ hath redeemed us from the curse of the law, *being made a curse FOR US:* for it is written, Cursed is every one that hangeth on a tree."

Yes, the Lord Jesus Christ saves the sinner from the guilt of sin because he took that guilt upon Himself, He bore the penalty of sin in His own body on the cross at Calvary. The curse He took was yours and mine. We were cursed because of sin. Jesus was God manifest in the flesh, He knew no sin but He was made to be sin because of us. He took our curse upon Himself and nailed it to the cross. Thus through His atoning death and the shedding of His precious blood our sin-debt was settled. God's wrath because of my sin, and because of your sin, was settled forever. Through faith in the death of Jesus, through faith in His finished work, my guilt was taken away and I have peace beyond all understanding! I can say today—and say from my heart —that I do not fear death, I have no fear of meeting God.

Why Jesus Christ Came Into the World

This is not a matter of theological opinion. It is a personal experience that I have had in my own heart. The Lord Jesus Christ saved me from the guilt and penalty of sin. I *know* He saved me, I do not just "think" or "hope" that I am saved. I know that Christ Jesus has power on earth to forgive sins. I know it because He has forgiven *my* sins and He lives in my heart today. I know that through His atoning death I am *delivered* from eternal death. I have accepted His shed blood as the grounds of my salvation, and every sin of mine has been blotted out forever.

Sinners Are Saved "FROM" and Saved "TO"

When the sinner believes on the Lord Jesus Christ, he is *saved FROM* the wrath to come: "Much more then, being now justified by His blood, we shall be saved from wrath through Him" (Rom. 5:9).

When the sinner is saved through faith in the finished work of Jesus he is *saved FROM* the curse of the broken law: "For as many as are of the works of the law are under the curse: for it is written, Cursed is every one that continueth not in all things which are written in the book of the law to do them" (Gal. 3:10).

The one who believes on Jesus is *saved FROM* the slavery of sin: "Know ye not, that to whom ye yield yourselves servants to obey, his servants ye are to whom ye obey; whether of sin unto death, or of obedience unto righteousness?" (Rom. 6:16).

When a sinner believes on Jesus, he is *saved FROM* the pollution of sin: "Know ye not that the unrighteous shall not inherit the kingdom of God? Be not deceived: neither fornicators, nor idolaters, nor adulterers, nor effeminate, nor abusers of themselves with mankind, nor thieves, nor covetous, nor drunkards, nor revilers, nor extortioners, shall inherit the kingdom of God" (I Cor. 6:9, 10).

The person who believes on Jesus is *saved FROM* the corruption of the world: "Whereby are given unto us exceeding great and precious promises: that by these ye might be partakers of the divine nature, having escaped the corruption that is in the world through lust" (II Pet. 1:4).

When a sinner believes on Jesus he is *saved FROM* the selfishness of self: "But chiefly them that walk after the flesh in the lust of uncleanness, and despise government. Presumptuous are they, selfwilled, they are not afraid to speak evil of dignities" (II Pet. 2:10).

Now let us look at some of the things *TO which* the sinner is saved when he believes on Jesus:

He is *saved TO* a new relationship with God: "As many as received Him, to them gave He power to become the sons of God, even to them that believe on His name" (John 1:12).

He is *saved TO* eternal life: "He that believeth on the Son hath everlasting life: and he that believeth not the Son shall not see life; but the wrath of God abideth on him" (John 3:36).

He is *saved TO* newness of life: "Therefore we are buried with Him by baptism into death: that like as Christ was raised up from the dead by the glory of the Father, even so we also should walk in newness of life" (Rom. 6:4).

He is *saved TO* holiness of character: "But now being made free from sin, and become servants to God, ye have your fruit unto holiness, and the end everlasting life" (Rom. 6:22).

He is *saved TO* purity of heart: "Blessed are the pure in heart: for they shall see God" (Matt. 5:8).

He is *saved TO* the love of Christ: "For the love of Christ constraineth us; because we thus judge, that if one died for all, then were all dead" (II Cor. 5:14).

He is *saved TO* sweetness of temper: "Let all bitterness, and wrath, and anger, and clamour, and evil speaking, be put away from you, with all malice: and be ye kind one to another, tender-hearted, forgiving one another, even as God for Christ's sake hath forgiven you" (Eph. 4:31, 32).

He is *saved TO* liberty and victory over Satan: "And they overcame him by the blood of the Lamb, and by the word of their testimony; and they loved not their lives unto the death" (Rev. 12:11).

All that salvation brings is by God's marvelous

grace: "Even when we were dead in sins, (He) hath quickened us together with Christ, (by grace ye are saved;) and hath raised us up together, and made us sit together in heavenly places in Christ Jesus: that in the ages to come He might shew the exceeding riches of His grace in His kindness toward us through Christ Jesus. For by grace are ye saved through faith; and that not of yourselves: it is the gift of God: not of works, lest any man should boast. For we are His workmanship, created in Christ Jesus unto good works, which God hath before ordained that we should walk in them" (Eph. 2:5-10).

Poor, helpless, hell-bound sinners are set free and sins atoned for by the blood of the Lamb: "Whom God hath set forth to be a propitiation through faith in His blood, to declare His righteousness for the remission of sins that are past, through the forbearance of God . . . that He might be just, and the Justifier of him which believeth in Jesus" (Rom. 3:25, 26).

We have life eternal, new life in Christ. Because He lives, we live: "And not only so, but we also joy in God through our Lord Jesus Christ, by whom we have now received the atonement" (Rom. 5:11).

I do not profess to understand it, but thank God I believe it! And among *the many things I do NOT know, I DO KNOW that I am saved by God's grace.* I am a new creation in Christ

Jesus, through faith in His shed blood:

"Therefore if any man be in Christ, he is a new creature: old things are passed away; behold, all things are become new. . . . For (God) hath made Him to be sin for us, who knew no sin; that we might be made the righteousness of God in Him" (II Cor. 5:17, 21).

The whole purpose of this message is to show that the Lord Jesus Christ left heaven with all of its glory, took upon Him a body of flesh, and came into this world in order to make salvation possible for you and for me.

Salvation is a tremendous word. The Greek words in our Bible which are translated "salvation" imply *deliverance, preservation, soundness, healing, safety.* Thus salvation speaks of all the redemptive acts of our Saviour concerning us—justification, redemption, propitiation, grace, forgiveness, imputation, sanctification, and glorification.

When the sinner believes on Jesus, he becomes a believer, saved from the *guilt and penalty* of sin. He becomes a child of God.

Then as the believer travels through this life, day by day and moment by moment he is kept by the power of God, saved from the *habits and power* of sin.

Finally, one glorious day Christ Jesus will come for His own and every believer will be caught out of this world, saved from the very *presence* of sin, to see sin no more!

This glorious salvation is by grace through faith, the gift of God, entirely without works. There is nothing the sinner can do to save himself, or to help God save him from sin. The sin-debt has been paid in full. Jesus came into the world to give His life a ransom for sinners. He was made to be sin for us, that we might be made the righteousness of God in Him. Therefore He paid the sin-debt, and a debt that is paid cannot be paid the second time. All God asks you and me to do is to have faith in the finished work of His Son. Believe on His name, trust in His shed blood, and God, for Christ's sake, will save—yes, to the uttermost—those who come unto Him through faith in Jesus.

Unbelieving friend, *God* has done all that He can do to keep you from spending eternity in hell. *Jesus* has done all that He can do to keep you out of hell. The *Holy Spirit* is doing all that He can do—yes, even this very moment He is convicting you of sin, calling you through this message, urging you to become a child of God. You have the Word of God, the Incorruptible Seed that brings saving faith. Therefore the Eternal Godhead has done everything possible to keep sinners out of hell. Now it is up to you to believe on Jesus, trust Him as your personal Saviour—and when you do that, God will forgive your sins and save you for Jesus' sake.

I have given my heart and life to Jesus. Have

Why Jesus Christ Came Into the World

YOU?   Are you a born again child of God?   If you are not, *you can be!*   Jesus came into the world to seek and to save sinners.   If you are a sinner, then He is *seeking you,* He is calling you through this message.   He is able, ready, willing, and anxious to save you this very moment.

Now let me give you some clear, understandable verses of Scripture that tell you how to be saved:

Paul and Silas were in jail in Philippi.   At midnight, as they prayed and sang praises to God, an earthquake opened the doors of the prison and loosed the chains from every prisoner.   The jailer, thinking his prisoners had fled, was about to take his own life; but Paul cried out, "Do thyself no harm, we are all here!"   Then calling for a light, the jailer came to Paul and Silas, fell down before them, and implored, "Sirs, what must I do to be saved?"   They replied, *"Believe on the Lord Jesus Christ, and thou shalt be saved,* and thy house."   Then "they spake unto him the Word of the Lord, and to all that were in his house" (Acts 16:25-32).

Listen to these words, do what they say, and you will be saved this very hour—and I will meet you in heaven, even though we may never meet on earth:

John 1:12, 13:   "As many as *received Him,* to them gave He power to become the sons of God, even to them that *believe on His name:* which were born, not of blood, nor of the will of the flesh, nor of the will of man, but of God."

John 3:18: "He that *believeth on Him* is not condemned: but he that believeth not is condemned already, because he hath not believed in the name of the only begotten Son of God."

John 3:36: "He that believeth on the Son *hath everlasting life:* and he that believeth not the Son shall not see life; but the wrath of God abideth on him."

John 5:24: "He that *heareth my Word,* and believeth on Him that sent me, *hath everlasting life,* and *shall not come into condemnation;* but *is passed* from death unto life."

Ephesians 2:8, 9: "*By GRACE* are ye saved *through faith;* and that not of yourselves: *it is the gift of God: NOT OF WORKS,* lest any man should boast."

Titus 3:5: "*Not by works of righteousness* which we have done, but *according to His mercy He saved us,* by the washing of regeneration, and renewing of the Holy Ghost."

Romans 10:13: "*Whosoever shall call* upon the name of the Lord *shall be saved.*"

Here are the words that changed me from a wretched, miserable sinner to a child of God. These are the words that changed my life:

"If thou shalt confess with thy mouth the Lord Jesus, and shalt believe in thine heart that God hath raised Him from the dead, *thou shalt be saved.* For with the heart man believeth unto righteousness; and with the mouth confession is

34

made unto salvation" (Rom. 10:9, 10).

Dear sinner, will you this moment bow your head, confess to Jesus that you believe these Scriptures to be true because His Word declares them to be so? Then in your own words ask Him to come into your heart, forgive your sins, and save your soul. And He will!

THE SINNER'S SIN—
THE SAVIOUR'S SACRIFICE

The Sinner's Sin—
The Saviour's Sacrifice

"As it is written, There is none righteous, no, not one. There is none that understandeth, there is none that seeketh after God. They are all gone out of the way, they are together become unprofitable; there is none that doeth good, no, not one. . . . For all have sinned, and come short of the glory of God" (Rom. 3:10-12, 23).

"For the law having a shadow of good things to come, and not the very image of the things, can never with those sacrifices which they offered year by year continually make the comers thereunto perfect. For then would they not have ceased to be offered? because that the worshippers once purged should have had no more conscience of sins. But in those sacrifices there is a remembrance again made of sins every year.

"For it is not possible that the blood of bulls and of goats should take away sins. Wherefore when He cometh into the world, He saith, Sacrifice and offering thou wouldest not, but a body hast thou prepared me. In burnt-offerings and sacrifices for sin thou hast had no pleasure. Then said I, Lo, I come (in the volume of the book it

39

is written of me,) to do thy will, O God.   Above when He said, Sacrifice and offering and burnt-offerings and offering for sin thou wouldest not, neither hadst pleasure therein; which are offered by the law.   Then said He, Lo, I come to do thy will, O God.   He taketh away the first, that He may establish the second.   By the which will we are sanctified through the offering of the body of Jesus Christ once for all.

"And every priest standeth daily ministering and offering oftentimes the same sacrifices, which can never take away sins: *but THIS MAN, after He had offered ONE SACRIFICE for sins for ever, sat down on the right hand of God"* (Heb. 10:1-12).

In this message we will study nine precious passages of Scripture, each of which presents two great truths: (1) the sins of the sinner, and (2) the all-sufficient sacrifice of the Saviour.

According to true Bible doctrine it is SIN (singular), not SINS (plural) that damns the sinner—"he that *believeth not* is *condemned already,* because he hath not believed in the name of the only begotten Son of God" (John 3:18b).   John the Baptist pointed Jesus out as "the Lamb of God, which taketh away *the SIN* of the world" (John 1:29).

The sin of unbelief (rejecting the Lord Jesus Christ) is enough to damn any soul—in fact, the sin of unbelief *has* damned every soul that burns in hell today.   But in this message we are going to deal with *sins* (plural). Jesus bore *all* sins, all *species* of sins. He "bare our sins in His own body on the tree, that we, being dead to sins, should live unto righteousness: by whose stripes ye were healed" (I Pet. 2:24). Therefore there is no excuse for anyone continuing in sin and plunging into hell.

And now the first of our nine passages of Scripture to be studied in this message:

1. *"Ye know that He was manifested to take away our sins; and in Him is no sin"* (I John 3:5).

To be "manifested" means to be *revealed* or *unveiled*. That is exactly what Jesus did. He revealed Himself "to take away our sins."

God's Christ had no beginning. He was in the beginning with God (John 1:1; 17:5). But in Genesis 3:15 God promised Adam that the seed of the woman would bruise (or crush) the serpent's head, and at the appointed time this promise was fulfilled: "When the fulness of the time was come, God sent forth His Son, made of a woman, made under the law, to redeem them that were under the law, that we might receive the adoption of sons" (Gal. 4:4, 5).

Yes, in the fulness of time Jesus left the Father's bosom, left heaven's glories to be born of the Virgin Mary. He took upon Himself a body like unto the body of man, sin apart; and in that body of flesh He revealed Himself: "The Word was made flesh, and dwelt among us, *and we beheld His glory, the glory as of the only begotten of the Father, full of grace and truth"* (John 1:14).

I John 3:5 clearly tells us that the only begotten Son of God appeared in human form for one specific purpose: to take away our sins. In I Timothy 3:16 Paul tells us, "Without controversy great is the mystery of godliness: God was manifest in the flesh, justified in the Spirit, seen of angels, preached unto the Gentiles, believed on in the world, received up into glory."

John the Beloved testifies, "The life was manifested, and we have seen it, and bear witness, and shew unto you that eternal life, which was with the Father, and was manifested unto us" (I John 1:2).

Christ was manifested to take away our sins by paying the sin-debt, and the only possible way the sin-debt could be paid was through death because "the wages of sin is death" (Rom. 6:23). ". . . sin, when it is finished, bringeth forth death" (James 1:15).

God's Christ was the only One who could pay the sin-debt because He alone knew no sin. God's holiness demands holiness, God's righteousness demands righteousness. Therefore He who knew no sin was made to be sin for us, "that we might be made the righteousness of God in Him" (II Cor. 5:21). Jesus did many things while He was here on earth. He healed the sick, opened the eyes of the blind, fed the hungry, performed many other miracles. But all that He did was secondary to the primary purpose of His coming into the world—i. e., to take away our sins through His atoning death on the cross.

Shall we *define* SIN? *What IS sin?* The Word of God answers in clear, understandable words:

All lawlessness is sin (I John 3:4; I Sam. 15:23, 24).

All unrighteousness is sin (I John 5:17).

Whatsoever is not of faith is sin (Rom. 14:23). An illustration of this is the offering Cain brought, as set forth in Hebrews 11:4.

The thought (or device) of foolishness is sin (Prov. 24:9). Korah furnishes a good example of this, as described in Numbers chapter 16.

A high look, a proud heart, and the plowing of the wicked is sin (Prov. 21:4). In other words, sin sums up the whole life of the natural man. Everything the unregenerate man does is sin.

To him that knoweth to do good and doeth it not, to him it is sin (James 4:17). Failing to do right is sin, just as surely as doing wrong is sin. Eli (I Sam. 3:13) is a good example of this.

Unbelief is the mother of all sin (John 16:9). Unbelief, as I have already stated, is the sin that has damned every soul that burns in hell, every soul that will plunge into hell between now and the consummation of all things.

Jesus fulfilled every jot and tittle of the law

(Matt. 5:17, 18). Therefore He is "made unto us wisdom, and righteousness, and sanctification, and redemption" (I Cor. 1:30). He completely satisfied the law of God, He satisfied the holiness of God, the righteousness of God, therefore He was eligible and qualified to pay sin's debt. The penalty of sin demanded death. Jesus died, laid His life down, that we might have life (John 10:18).

2. *"THIS MAN, after He had offered one sacrifice for sins FOR EVER, sat down on the right hand of God" (Heb. 10:12).*

During the Old Testament era, there were tens of thousands of animals slain and barrels of blood shed because of sacrifices offered for sins; but these sacrifices could not take away sins. "For it is not possible that the blood of bulls and of goats should take away sins" (Heb. 10:4). But in the fulness of time "this Man," the God-Man, came into the world to offer the one sacrifice that would satisfy God and *take away* sins—one sacrifice for sins forever. Jesus offered *ONE offering*, never to be repeated. The one offering He made, the offering of Himself, was, is, and forever will be sufficient to meet the need of every sinner who comes to God in the name of Jesus. It matters not how many sins one may have committed or how wretched the sinner may be, the one sacrifice Jesus offered is all-sufficient to save any and all who come unto God by Him.

The Sinner's Sin—The Saviour's Sacrifice

During the Old Testament era, the priest offered sacrifices again and again, many times the same sacrifice for the same sin; and when a priest died, his priesthood ceased to be. But not so with our Great High Priest: *"This Man,* because He continueth ever, hath *an unchangeable priesthood.* Wherefore He is able also to save them to the uttermost that come unto God by Him, seeing He ever liveth to make intercession for them" (Heb. 7:24, 25).

If I can get one soul to see and accept the truth of these words, this message will not be in vain. Jesus Christ, only begotten Son of God, offered Himself—one sacrifice, offered one time, for all, forever, never to be repeated. Therefore when a sinner recognizes the Saviour as the sinless sacrifice and receives the Lord Jesus Christ, that very moment the blood of Jesus cleanses the sinner from all sin (and sins, as those sins are confessed to Him).

Every born again believer possesses within his heart the Christ who offered the one sacrifice. He does not offer sacrifice for us, because He abides within us—Christ in you, the hope of glory (Col. 1:27). "There is therefore now no condemnation to them which are in Christ Jesus. . . . If any man have not the Spirit of Christ, he is none of His. . . . For as many as are led by the Spirit of God, they are the sons of God" (Rom. 8:1, 9, 14).

II Peter 1:3, 4 tells us that God has given unto

us "all things that pertain unto life and godliness, through the knowledge of Him that hath called us to glory and virtue: whereby are given unto us exceeding great and precious promises: that by these ye might be partakers of the divine nature, having escaped the corruption that is in the world through lust."

I Corinthians 10:13 assures us, "There hath no temptation taken you but such as is common to man: but God is faithful, who will not suffer you to be tempted above that ye are able; but will with the temptation also make a way to escape, that ye may be able to bear it."

Therefore, believers can say with the Apostle Paul, *"In all these things we are more than conquerors through Him that loved us!"* (Rom. 8:37).

In Hebrews, the Holy Spirit repeats again and again the words *"one"* and *"once"*:

"Neither by the blood of goats and calves, but *by His own blood He entered in ONCE into the holy place,* having obtained eternal redemption for us. . . . For then must He often have suffered since the foundation of the world: but now *ONCE in the end of the world hath He appeared* to put away sin by the sacrifice of Himself. . . . So Christ was ONCE offered to bear the sins of many; and unto them that look for Him shall He appear the second time without sin unto salvation" (Heb. 9:12, 26, 28).

"Then said He, Lo, I come to do thy will, O

46

God. He taketh away the first, that He may establish the second. By the which will we are sanctified through the offering of the body of Jesus Christ *ONCE for all"* (Heb. 10:9,10).

What a contrast between the one offering of Jesus and the many offerings offered by many priests in the days of the Mosaic economy! The very fact that these sacrifices were offered over and over proclaims their imperfection. But in Jesus we see the perfect sacrifice—the sacrifice of Himself. God accepted the perfect offering of His Son, the Lamb without blemish and without spot; and when we receive Jesus as our Saviour, God saves us for Jesus' sake (Eph. 4:32). Therefore when we stand before God we will stand in the perfection of the blood of Jesus, and He will confess us to the Father because He is our Saviour and we are His children.

3. *"Grace be to you and peace from God the Father, and from our Lord Jesus Christ, who gave Himself for our sins, that He might deliver us from this present evil world, according to the will of God and our Father"* (Gal. 1:3, 4).

Jesus came into the world to give His life a ransom for many. He lived His earthly life on our behalf, and on our behalf He took the punishment our sin (and sins) demanded. He consecrated His will to the Father's will, and every moment He lived on this earth was dedicated to the Father's will in paying sin's debt.

His earthly life can be summed up in one word: *OBEDIENCE.* He obeyed the Father's command in everything. He moved as the Father ordered, He spoke as the Father dictated. The miracles He performed were wrought under the Father's direction. Nothing He said or did was in the interest of self-gain. Always He set forth the truth that He came from God to do the will of God and to give His life a ransom for sinners. In John 8:28, 29 He declared:

"When ye have lifted up the Son of man, then shall ye know that I am He, and that I do nothing of myself; but as my Father hath taught me, I speak these things. And He that sent me is with me: the Father hath not left me alone; for I do always those things that please Him!"

In John 17:4 He said to the heavenly Father, "I have glorified thee on the earth: I have finished the work which thou gavest me to do."

God the Father so loved the world that He gave His only begotten Son to die for the sins of the world—but never entertain the thought that Jesus was *forced* to die. He gave Himself for us. He willingly laid His life down that we might have life and have it abundantly (John 10:10, 18). Christ's death was voluntary. There was no compulsion laid upon Him save the impulsion of His own heart of love for sinners. Love compels by impelling. There is no other power that moves as mightily as love, and there is no love as powerful as the love of God and God's Christ. In the following verses, the words "gave" and "give" illustrate the ministry of the Holy Spirit in pointing out that Christ's death was voluntary:

He "GAVE Himself for our sins, that He might deliver us from this present evil world, according to the will of God and our Father" (Gal. 1:4).

"I am crucified with Christ: nevertheless I live; yet not I, but Christ liveth in me: and the life which I now live in the flesh I live by the faith of the Son of God, *who loved me, and GAVE Himself for me*" (Gal. 2:20).

He "GAVE Himself a ransom for all, to be testified in due time" (I Tim. 2:6).

". . . Christ also loved the Church, and *GAVE Himself for it*" (Eph. 5:25).

He *"GAVE Himself for us*, that He might redeem us from all iniquity, and purify unto Himself a peculiar people, zealous of good works" (Tit. 2:14).

". . . the Son of man came not to be ministered unto, but to minister, and *to GIVE His life* a ransom for many" (Matt. 20:28).

". . . the Good Shepherd *GIVETH His life* for the sheep" (John 10:11).

These passages show Christ's willingness to die to deliver us from the wages of sin. He willingly took a body of flesh and in that body He met the devil face to face. He was tempted in all points as we are tempted, He battled the tempter in our stead, and He conquered the world, the flesh, the devil, death, hell, and the grave that we might be more than conquerors!

Romans 8:34 asks, "Who is he that condemneth?" It is Christ that died, yea rather, that is risen again, who is even at the right hand of God, who also maketh intercession for us." According to these words, if I go to hell it will be Jesus who condemns me to that place. But I know that Jesus will never condemn me to the pits of the damned because He is my Saviour. He abides in my bosom, I am His child. I am hid with Christ in God. Jesus is my Mediator, my Confessor. He lives to make intercession for me. I love Him, and He loves me. Perfect love casteth out fear, therefore I am not afraid to die, I am not afraid to stand before God. My Saviour has promised to go with me even unto the end; and since I have confessed Him before men He will confess me before the heavenly Father.

Have YOU confessed Jesus as your Saviour? He gave Himself for your sins, it is not His will that you perish. Therefore if you are not a Christian, bow your head this moment and receive Jesus by faith. Allow Him to come into your heart in the Person of the Holy Spirit. He will save you, and your heart will bear witness that you are a child of God.

4. *"He is the propitiation for our sins: and not for our's only, but also for the sins of the whole world" (I John 2:2).*

Christ does not save the sinner and then leave him to fight his own battles. Redemption is but the beginning of salvation—that is, when one believes on Jesus for the remission of sin, that individual is just as perfectly *redeemed* as he will ever be. But that is only the beginning. We are saved from the penalty of sin when we believe, but we are also delivered day by day from temptation and the power of sin as we trust and feed on the Word of God. Jesus does not want us to sin. He wants us to glorify Him in all that we do. But *"IF any man sin,* we have an Advocate with the Father, Jesus Christ the righteous" (I John 2:1).

Jesus is eligible to be our Advocate and Mediator because He is the Righteous One. In Him there is no sin, therefore He can approach the Father in our behalf:

'For there is one God, and one Mediator between God and men, the Man Christ Jesus" (I Tim. 2:5). It is by the blood of Jesus that we have "boldness to enter into the holiest . . . by a new and living way, which He hath consecrated for us through the veil, that is to say, His flesh" (Heb. 10:19, 20).

Our Perfect Salvation

Everything having to do with our salvation

51

is in Jesus. We are complete in Him. He is the Alpha and Omega, the Author and Finisher of all that has to do with our arrival in heaven.

Christ is our Mediator, and the Greek language concerning mediation signifies "by means of; a procuring cause which brings something to someone else." I hope you will read and study the following Scriptures which clearly show that it is *by means of* the life, death, burial, resurrection, and ascension of the Lord Jesus Christ that we possess this glorious salvation:

Through Jesus we have *salvation*—He came into the world that through Him we might be saved (John 3:17; 10:9).

Through Jesus we are God's *purchased possession*—purchased with His own blood (Acts 20:28).

Through Jesus we *approach God*—no man can come to the Father but by the Son (John 14:6).

Through Jesus, through His blood, we have *redemption* (Eph. 1:7).

Through Jesus we have *reconciliation*—we are "reconciled to God by the death of His Son" (Rom. 5:10).

Through Jesus we have *righteousness*—by His obedience "shall many be made righteous" (Rom. 5:19).

Through Jesus we have *victory* (Rom. 8:37; I Cor. 15:57).

Through Jesus we are assured of *resurrection*—"as in Adam all die, even so in Christ shall all be made alive" (I Cor. 15:22).

Through Jesus we have *adoption*—we are "predestinated . . . unto the adoption of children" (Eph. 1:5).

Through Jesus we have *access* "by one Spirit *unto the Father*" (Eph. 2:18).

Through Jesus we have *peace*—He "made peace through the blood of His cross" (Col. 1:20).

Through Jesus we have *atonement*—"He . . . by Himself purged our sins" (Heb. 1:3).

Through Jesus we have *deliverance*—through death He destroyed "him that had the power of death, that is, the devil," and delivered "them who through fear of death were all their lifetime subject to bondage" (Heb. 2:14, 15).

Through Jesus we have *sanctification*—"we are sanctified through the offering of the body of Jesus Christ once for all" (Heb. 10:10). He "suffered without the gate" that He might sanctify us "with His own blood" (Heb. 13:12).

The Lord Jesus Christ is *all I need*, He is all *you* need. There is no other Saviour, no other Mediator between God and men. We are warned, "Beware lest any man spoil you through philosophy and vain deceit, after the tradition of men, after the rudiments of the world, and not after Christ. *For in Him dwelleth all the fulness of the Godhead bodily, and YE ARE COMPLETE IN HIM, which is the head of all principality and power*" (Col. 2:8-10).

5. *"For Christ also hath once suffered for sins, the Just for the unjust, that He might bring us to God, being put to death in the flesh, but quickened by the Spirit"* (I Pet. 3:18).

Here the Apostle Peter points out that Jesus suffered for sins—but not for His own sins because there was no sin in Him. He was the Sinless One. He was the Just One suffering for the unjust.

Even those who were not followers of Jesus declared that He was sinless. Pilate confessed, "I find in Him no fault at all. . . . I find no fault in Him. . . . Take ye Him and crucify Him, for I find no fault in Him" (John 18:38; 19:4, 6).

The thief on the cross, he who listened to Jesus and later asked to be remembered when the Lord came into His kingdom, testified, "We receive the due reward of our deeds; *but THIS MAN hath done nothing amiss"* (Luke 23:41). The same Greek word here translated "amiss" is rendered "harm" in Acts 28:6, and in II Thessalonians 3:2 it is translated "unreasonable." There was nothing *amiss* in Christ's character, there was no *harm* in His actions, there was nothing *unreasonable* in His teaching. He challenged His enemies, "Which of you convinceth me of sin?" (John 8:46). No man could point to anything amiss or sinful in the life of Jesus.

I Peter 2:22 tells us that Jesus "did no sin, neither was guile found in His mouth."

I John 3:5 tells us that not only was Jesus manifested *to take away our sins,* but also *"in Him IS NO SIN."*

In II Corinthians 5:21 the Apostle Paul tells us that Jesus knew no sin, but was made to be sin *for US,* "that we might be made the righteousness of God in Him."

In Hebrews 7:26 we read that Jesus, our High Priest, "is holy, harmless, undefiled, separate from sinners, and made higher than the heavens."

Those who followed Him day by day confessed that He did all things well, and even the officers who were sent to arrest Him as a disturber of the peace returned to the chief priests and Pharisees and declared, "Never man spake *like this Man"* (John 7:46).

When Jesus was finally arrested and brought before Pilate, the governor's wife sent him a message, saying, *"Have thou nothing to do with that JUST MAN:* for I have suffered many things this day in a dream because of Him" (Matt. 27:19).

During the years of my ministry I have had many people come to me and say, "You make salvation too easy! You invite people to trust Jesus, believe on Him, and be saved. That is entirely too simple." Beloved, *salvation IS simple!* It is easy to understand. What do I tell these dear souls who complain that I make it too simple? I tell them that there is enough Gospel in John 3:16—or in Ephesians 2:8 or Acts 16:31—to save *the entire world* if the world would only *believe* those verses.

But remember—even though salvation is simply *trusting Jesus,* the *cost* of salvation was great, *more than ANY MAN could pay.* Jesus *paid* this tremendous price in order for salvation to be simple and easy for *us,* and the glorious verses that tell us of salvation—the gift of God by faith in the finished work of Jesus—were made possible through the death of the Son of God, the Sinless One who came into the world to die, that He might bring us to God! Reflect for a moment, my friend: It took every pain Jesus suffered, every burden He carried, every tear He shed, every insult that was heaped upon Him to make John 3:16 possible.

> *Jesus paid it all—*
> *All to Him I owe.*
> *Sin had left a crimson stain—*
> *He washed it white as snow!*

6. *"So Christ was once offered to bear the sins of many; and unto them that look for Him shall He appear the second time without sin unto salvation" (Heb. 9:28).*

In this verse we have a magnificent picture of what Christ did for us. *"To bear"* means "to bring, to carry, or to lead up." In the Old Testament economy, the offering (an animal or dove) was brought or led to the altar of sacrifice. Jesus the Lamb of God was brought (or led) "as a lamb to the slaughter" and our sins were laid on Him

56

(Isa. 53:6, 7). There was no sin in Him, but He was *our sacrifice.* He bore *our sins* in His own body on the cross. He declared:

"As Moses lifted up the serpent in the wilderness, even so must the Son of man be lifted up: that whosoever believeth in Him should not perish, but have eternal life" (John 3:14, 15).

"And I, if I be lifted up from the earth, will draw all men unto me" (John 12:32).

Jesus bore our sins and made the sacrifice and offering that satisfied God. The sin-offering in the Old Testament economy is typical of Christ in His answering to God for our sins—and *sin* as well. By Jesus the Lamb, God dealt with our sin in judgment. Christ was made to be sin for us, He was made a curse in bearing the penalty of the broken law (Deut. 21:23; Gal. 3:13). He was condemned on our account (Rom. 8:3), stricken on our behalf (Isa. 53:8).

Sin is the root, *sins* the fruit. *Sin* is the source of all iniquity, and *lawlessness* is the stream that flows from the fountain of sin. *Sin* is the state, *sins* are the acts. *Sin* is the nature, *sins* are the life of the unregenerate. *Sin* is the inward condition, *sins* are the outward manifestation of evil in the life of the unbeliever. Therefore Christ has answered for our *sin* and our *sins.*

Christ was "offered *to bear the sins of MANY.*" How thankful I am that He did not bear just the sins of a select, elect minority! God's Word plainly tells us that *He is "the propitiation for OUR sins*—and not for our's *only,* but also *for the sins of the whole world"* (I John 2:2). All are included, not one is excluded. Jesus died for the sins of the world, and whosoever shall call upon the name of the Lord shall be saved.

The sin-question is settled. Now it is the Son-question: "What think ye of *Christ? Whose Son is He?"* If you will confess that Jesus is the Son of God, and believe in your heart that God sent Him into the world to die for your sins; to bear your sins in His body on the cross; that He was crucified, buried, and that He rose again the third day, God will save you for Jesus' sake:

"If thou shalt confess with thy mouth the Lord Jesus, and shalt believe in thine heart that God hath raised Him from the dead, thou shalt be saved. For with the heart man believeth unto righteousness; and with the mouth confession is made unto salvation" (Rom. 10:9, 10).

7. *Jesus "His own self bare our sins in His own body on the tree, that we, being dead to sins, should live unto righteousness: by whose stripes ye were healed" (I Pet. 2:24).*

Jesus wrapped up the Word in flesh and brought God down to man:

"In the beginning was the Word, and the Word was with God, and the Word was God. The same was in the beginning with God. . . . And the Word was made flesh, and dwelt among us, (and we beheld His glory, the glory as of the only begotten of the Father,) full of grace and truth" (John 1:1, 2, 14).

"God was in Christ, reconciling the world unto Himself . . ." (II Cor. 5:19).

Jesus took a body in order to suffer and die for our sins. Hebrews 10:4-10 explains it in these words:

"For it is not possible that the blood of bulls and of goats should take away sins. Wherefore when He cometh into the world, He saith: Sacrifice and offering thou wouldest not, but a body hast thou prepared me. In burnt-offerings and sacrifices for sin thou hast had no pleasure. Then said I, Lo, I come (in the volume of the book it is written of me,) to do thy will, O God. Above when He said, Sacrifice and offering and burnt-offerings and offering for sin thou wouldest not, neither hadst pleasure therein; which are offered by the law. Then said He, Lo, I come to do thy will, O God. He taketh away the first, that He may establish the second. By the which will we are sanctified through the offering of the body of Jesus Christ once for all."

It was a divine imperative that Jesus take a body of flesh in order to pay sin's debt. The wages of sin is death, and God cannot die. God is an eternal Spirit (John 4:24) and it is therefore impossible for Him to die. Jesus took a body that by the grace of God He might taste death for every man (Heb. 2:9). As Paul wrote to the Philippian believers, Jesus "being in the *form* of God thought it not robbery to be *equal* with God: but *made Himself of no reputation, and took upon Him the form of a servant, and was made in the likeness of men:* and being found in fashion as a man, He humbled Himself, and became obedient unto death, even the death of the cross" (Phil. 2:6-8).

We have already noted that the offerings and sacrifices made during the Old Testament era under the law could not take away sins. The law was not *given* to take away sins. By the law is the *knowledge* of sin, but by the *deeds* of the law no flesh shall be justified in the sight of God (Rom. 3:20). Therefore—"what the law could not do, in that it was weak through the flesh, God sending His own Son in the *likeness* of sinful flesh, and for sin, condemned sin in the flesh, that the righteousness of the law might be fulfilled in us, who walk not after the flesh, but after the Spirit" (Rom. 8:3, 4).

Sin and death are synonymous, and in order for Jesus to take the sinner's place it was necessary for Him to die. In order for Him to die it was necessary that He take a body of flesh like unto our body, sin apart. This He did; and as through one man's disobedience death moved upon all men, through the *obedience* of the Lord Jesus

Christ many are delivered from the wages of sin, set free from sin's penalty through faith in the finished work of Jesus who bore our sins in His own body on the tree:

"Wherefore, as by one man sin entered into the world, and death by sin; and so death passed upon all men, for that all have sinned. . . . But not as the offence, so also is the free gift. For if through the offence of one many be dead, much more the grace of God, and the gift by grace, which is by one Man, Jesus Christ, hath abounded unto many. And not as it was by one that sinned, so is the gift: for the judgment was by one to condemnation, but the free gift is of many offences unto justification.

"For if by one man's offence death reigned by one; much more they which receive abundance of grace and of the gift of righteousness shall reign in life by One, Jesus Christ. Therefore as by the offence of one judgment came upon all men to condemnation; even so by the righteousness of One the free gift came upon all men unto justification of life.

"For as by one man's disobedience many were made sinners, so by the obedience of One shall many be made righteous. Moreover the law entered, that the offence might abound. But where sin abounded, grace did much more abound: that as sin hath reigned unto death, even so might grace reign through righteousness unto eternal life by Jesus Christ our Lord" (Rom. 5:12, 15-21).

Dear friend, *are YOU saved?* If not, what a tragedy! Jesus bore your sins, He nailed them to the cross when He died at Calvary. He paid your sin-debt in full. Now what a tragedy it would be for you to die in sin and spend eternity in hell, when all that is necessary for you to be delivered from the wages of sin is for you to receive the Lord Jesus Christ, believe on Him, and let Him save your soul!

8. *"This is my blood of the new testament, which is shed for many for the remission of sins"* *(Matt. 26:28).*

Many books have been written about the Lord Jesus Christ—why He came into the world, what He did, who He was. Tens of thousands of sermons have been preached about Him. But His mission on earth can be summed up in the words of the verse just quoted: He came to die on a cross, to be lifted up from the earth, *to shed His blood for the remission of sins.*

Jesus was born to die. He took a body of flesh in order to die. His blood was destined to be shed for the remission of the sins of the world. From the moment He was born His face was set toward Calvary.

"Remission" means to free one who is a captive, the setting free of a slave. All unregenerate men are captives of Satan, slaves under sin, until

Jesus sets them free. We are by nature the children of wrath (Eph. 2:3), born in sin and shapen in iniquity (Psalm 51:5). We are born in a body that is determined to damn us, we live in a *world* that is determined to damn us, and we are followed by the devil who, "as a roaring lion, walketh about, seeking whom he may devour" (I Pet. 5:8). We can escape the damnation of hell only because Jesus conquered the world, the flesh, and the devil!

Without Shedding of Blood, No Remission

In this day of liberalism and modernism, many shudder when God's preachers mention the blood atonement. "Slaughterhouse preachers," they call them. But I declare on the authority of God's infallible Word that *apart from the shedding of the blood of Jesus there IS no remission for sin:*

"Almost all things are by the law purged with blood; and *without* shedding of blood *is no remission*" (Heb. 9:22).

"Forasmuch as ye know that ye were not redeemed with corruptible things, as silver and gold, from your vain conversation received by tradition from your fathers; but with *the precious blood of Christ,* as of a lamb without blemish and without spot: who verily was foreordained before the foundation of the world, but was manifest in these last times for you" (I Pet. 1:18-20).

"If we walk in the light, as He is in the light,

we have fellowship one with another, and *the blood of Jesus Christ His Son cleanseth us from all sin"* (I John 1:7).

It matters not what men think about the blood of Jesus, it matters not what preachers preach about it. The important thing is *what the Word of God declares about it.* And I declare without apology that unless a man is cleansed by the blood, redeemed by the blood, he will spend eternity in hell—and when I say hell, I am referring to the lake that burns with fire and brimstone!

Blessings That Come
Only Through the Blood of Jesus

I urge you to read and study the following Scriptures which point out fourteen distinct blessings which come to the believer through the blood of the Lord Jesus Christ:

Remission of sins (Matt. 26:28).

Redemption (Eph. 1:7; Col. 1:14; I Pet. 1:19).

Reconciliation (Col. 1:20).

Justification (Rom. 5:9).

Conscience purged from dead works (Heb. 9:14).

Black heart washed white (Rev. 7:14).

Access into the holiest (Heb. 10:19).

Nearness to God (Eph. 2:13).

Freedom from sin (Rev. 1:5).

Sanctification (Heb. 13:12).

Cleansing (I John 1:7).

God's purchased possession (Acts 20:28).

Communion with God and Christ (I Cor. 10:16).

Victory over the world, the flesh, and the devil (Rev. 12:11).

The only guarantee for heaven is the covering of the blood of Jesus. *Are YOU washed in the blood?* If not, you are still in your sins, and apart from the precious blood of Jesus there is no remission from sin!

9. *"I delivered unto you first of all that which I also received, how that Christ died for our sins according to the Scriptures" (I Cor. 15:3).*

The message Paul delivered was the message he received, the message God gave him on the Damascus road when the light from heaven struck him down and he asked, "Who art thou, Lord?" The answer came back, "I am Jesus whom thou persecutest." (You will find the account of Paul's conversion in Acts 9:1-20.) From that day forward, Saul of Tarsus, now become Paul the Apostle, preached *Jesus* — but not according to Judaism, not according to "religion." He preached Jesus *according to the Scriptures.*

Christ died as no other man ever died. He died "according to the Scriptures," and the only place where we can learn the truth about the death of Jesus and His mission on earth is in *the source of all truth* — the Word of God. Jesus is the *living* Word (John 1:1), Jesus is truth (John 14:6).

What Do the Scriptures Reveal
Concerning the Death of Christ?

The Word of God teaches that the death of Christ was *divine in its provision:*

God is light (I John 1:5). God is love (I John 4:8). Both of these divine facts shine out at Calvary. Since God is light He cannot pass over sin, nor can He allow sin to go unpunished. Therefore at Calvary the love of God is on display because in Jesus He provided what He demanded to pay the sin-debt. The death of Jesus at Calvary was the crowning act of a holy God:

"For God so loved the world, that He gave His only begotten Son, that whosoever believeth in Him should not perish, but have everlasting life" (John 3:16).

"God commendeth His love toward us, in that, while we were yet sinners, Christ died for us" (Rom. 5:8).

"Greater love hath no man than this, that a man lay down his life for his friends" (John 15:13). But Christ laid down His life for His enemies, for those who hated Him. Everything about Christ's death on Calvary is the manifestation of love.

The Word of God teaches that the death of Christ was *essential in its necessity:*

When the Scripture says "must," *it means "MUST"!* Jesus declared, "As Moses lifted up the serpent in the wilderness, *even so MUST the Son of man be lifted up"* (John 3:14).

In John 12:32 He said, "And I, if I be lifted up from the earth, will draw all men unto me." Thus did He signify what death He would die.

The virgin birth of Jesus was not enough. His sinless life was not enough. His ministry was not enough. His miracles were not enough. In order to save men from sin it was a divine necessity that He die on the cross.

Some people declare that if a person is sincere in what he believes, whatever his religion may be, that religion is just as good as Christianity. They say that Mohammed, Confucius, and other great religious leaders were just as great as Jesus. The various religions of the world were founded by the men whose names they bear, and almost all of these great men are dead—but not one of them has ever come back from the grave! Only the Lord Jesus Christ returned to this earth from the grave, and He gave indisputable proof of His resurrection (Acts 1:3). Christ is not the "Founder" of Christianity, *He IS Christianity!* Christianity is *Christ in the believer* (Col. 1:27).

Man cannot bring himself to God. It is Jesus who draws men to God. The inability of man to save himself has been demonstrated since the Garden of Eden. The Bible clearly teaches, "That which is crooked cannot be made straight, and that which is wanting cannot be numbered" (Eccl. 1:15). Jesus Himself declared, "A good tree cannot bring forth evil fruit, neither can a corrupt tree bring forth good fruit" (Matt. 7:18).

Like produces like. Jesus said to Nicodemus, "That which is born of the flesh is flesh; and that which is born of the Spirit is spirit" (John 3:6). Therefore, *"Ye must be born again"* (John 3:7). To His disciples Jesus said, "Abide in me, and I in you. As the branch cannot bear fruit of itself, except it abide in the vine; no more can ye, except ye abide in me" (John 15:4). "They that are in the flesh cannot please God" (Rom. 8:8), and sacrifices and rituals can never take away sin (Heb. 10:11).

Churches are filled today with people who think that religious acts, good living, will avail for the removal of their sins; but when they stand before God they will discover that only the blood of Jesus can take away sins! Yes, the death of Jesus was essential in its necessity.

The Word of God teaches that the death of Jesus was *voluntary:*

The death of Jesus was not an accident, nor did He die a martyr's death. He laid His life down, willingly. No man took it from Him. There was no compulsion, there was only the impulsion of His own love that caused Him to lay His life down for us. *Four times* in the tenth chapter of John's Gospel He tells us that He *gave* His life, laid it down willingly:

"The Good Shepherd *giveth* His life for the sheep. . . . I *lay down* my life for the sheep. . . . I

lay down my life. . . . I *lay it down of myself*"
(John 10:11, 15, 17, 18).

The Word of God teaches that the death of
Christ was *substitutionary in its offering:*

The Holy Spirit declares that the definition
of the Gospel is the death, burial, and resurrection
of the Lord Jesus Christ (I Cor. 15:1-4). He died
for our sins "according to the Scriptures." There
were sins to die for, and on the cross He bore
our sins. He finished what He came into the
world to do. He came to die for the sins of the
world, to give His life a ransom for many, to shed
His blood for the remission of sins. Just before
He committed His spirit back to the Father He
proclaimed from the cross, "It is finished!" (John
19:30). God's Anointed One was sent into the
world to accomplish a work, and He finished it
alone. Nothing can be added to what He com-
pleted so perfectly. There is therefore no more
offering for sin. Christ offered the one sacrifice—
once, for all, forever, never to be repeated—and
even if there was a *need* to add to the sacrifice
He made, *no man* could make that addition! Since
there *is* no such need, what foolishness and folly
for man to attempt to add to that which God finished perfectly in the death of His Son on Calvary!

The Word of God teaches that the death of
Christ was *sufficient in its atonement:*

In John 6:55 Jesus declared, "My flesh is *meat*
indeed, and my blood is *drink* indeed." Here He

sets forth the two material things which satisfy the hunger of the body. In like manner, the death of Christ meets the need and satisfies the hunger of the sin-conscious soul. Furthermore, His death brings salvation and meets the claims of God the Father, to His satisfaction and delight. In Matthew 3:17 God audibly declared, "This is my beloved Son, in whom I am *well pleased.*" Again in Matthew 17:5 He audibly said, "This is my beloved Son, in whom I am *well pleased; hear ye Him.*"

Yes, the death of Jesus on the cross was sufficient in its atonement—sufficient to bring salvation to the believer and satisfaction and delight to the heavenly Father. We have peace with God by means of the blood of Jesus. Hell is defeated by His blood and heaven is made certain for believers by the passport of the blood. We are complete in Him—and nothing can be added to completeness.

The Word of God teaches us that the death of Christ was *complete in its issue:*

All hell could not stop the heart of Jesus nor take His spirit from His body. His life could not depart this earth until He Himself declared that His work on earth was finished. The law of God was magnified and satisfied. The justice of God was satisfied. Now God can be just and yet justify the ungodly—but He can do this only through the blood of Jesus.

In the death of Jesus, God was glorified.

In the death of Jesus, the Scriptures were fulfilled.

In the death of Jesus, sin's damnation was defeated and removed.

All who believe are delivered from sin—but only through Calvary.

All spiritual blessings are secured by means of His death on Calvary. He said, "Except a corn of wheat fall into the ground and die, it abideth alone: but if it die, it bringeth forth much fruit" (John 12:24).

According to the teaching of liberals and modernists, the remission of sins does not depend upon the blood of Christ, but rather that men obtain remission through the incorporation of *His* life with the life of man, as man strives to follow His example. But this is not what the Word of God teaches. Jesus did not come into the world to be our example, and regardless of how sincerely we strive to live as He lived, this will not bring remission of sin. Hope for hell-deserving sinners lies in these divine facts:

Christ died for our sins.

He bore our sins in His own body on the cross.

He was manifested to take away our sins.

He appeared to put away sin by the sacrifice of Himself.

Christ died for the ungodly.

The message of Christ crucified "according to the Scriptures" dispels all darkness, kills all sin, answers all questions, defeats all foes, removes all fears, satisfies hunger and thirst, meets every hope, fulfills every longing of the human heart, and keeps every promise.

Are you saved according to "Thus saith the Lord"? Have you been born again, born from above? Jesus said, "Except ye repent ye shall all likewise perish" (Luke 13:3, 5). Have you repented in sincerity? If not, you are lost, and unless you repent and come to Jesus for salvation you will one day perish eternally in the lake of fire!

In Closing

In this message I have given nine Scriptures dealing with the sinner's sin and the Saviour's sacrifice. Now let me give these same Scriptures in a nutshell:

1. Jesus was manifested to take away our sins (I John 3:5).
2. He was offered—one sacrifice for sins (Heb. 10:12).
3. He gave Himself for our sins (Gal. 1:4).
4. He is the propitiation for our sins (I John 2:2).
5. He suffered for sins, the Just for the unjust (I Pet. 3:18).
6. He was once offered to bear the sins of many (Heb. 9:28).
7. He bore our sins in His own body on the tree (I Pet. 2:24).
8. He shed His blood for the remission of sins

(Matt. 26:28).

9. He died for our sins according to the Scriptures (I Cor. 15:3).

Jesus paid it ALL! Salvation is God's gift to you and to me. I have received His finished work by faith. *Have YOU?* If you have not, I urge you this very moment to bow your head and in your own words talk to God and tell Him that you do believe He so loved you that He gave His only begotten Son to die for you, and that you now receive Jesus as your Saviour. If you will do this, God will save you for Jesus' sake:

"Be ye kind one to another, tenderhearted, forgiving one another, even as *God for Christ's sake hath forgiven you*" (Eph. 4:32).

"I write unto you, little children, because *your sins are forgiven you for His name's sake*" (I John 2:12).

ETERNAL LIFE A PRESENT POSSESSION

Eternal Life a Present Possession

"These things have I written unto you that believe on the name of the Son of God; *that ye may KNOW that ye have eternal life,* and that ye may believe on the name of the Son of God" (I John 5:13).

"Religion" has done an excellent job of confusing people about salvation and what salvation does for those who possess it. We hear people pray, "Lord, *at last* save us in heaven," or "Lord, deliver us until the bitter end *and then* receive us unto thyself." Many other similar prayers are prayed by church people. Such inexcusable Bible ignorance is indeed sad, because the Word of God so clearly sets forth the assurance that *believers possess eternal life NOW*—and this assurance is separate and apart from feelings (emotions).

There is much confusion, even among born again believers, concerning salvation and the emotions which occur either at the *time* of salvation or immediately following that moment. Therefore I ask you to bear this in mind, beloved: *nothing changes more rapidly than our personal feelings,* whereas the Word of God is forever settled in heaven, and *it never changes!* I dogmatically declare that the person who is a possessor of eternal life does not just "hope" or "think" he is saved, *he KNOWS* he possesses eternal life and that he is saved by the grace of God. In this message we will study Scriptures that prove beyond any shadow of doubt that when one is truly saved, a possessor of eternal life, he knows it just as surely as he knows he is alive physically.

Eternal Life Is the Gift of God

"I give unto them eternal life; and they shall never perish, neither shall any man pluck them out of my hand" (John 10:28).

"The thief cometh not, but for to steal, and to kill, and to destroy. *I am come that they might have life,* and that they might have it more abundantly" (John 10:10).

Eternal life is ours—not through baptism, good works, good living, not through "quitting" this or that—but through Jesus Christ our Lord, and *only* through Him. How wonderful is the gift God provided, the gift of eternal life offered to *"whosoever will."*

The night I was saved, the minister took his text from Romans 6:23: *"The WAGES of sin is death: but the GIFT OF GOD is eternal life through Jesus Christ our Lord."* I stood in the doorway of a little country church that night as God's humble pastor opened the Word of God and delivered a message from that verse of Scripture, a message that reached my heart. He proved to me that as a sinner I would receive wages—and the wages would be eternal damnation in hell. Then—also from the Word of God—step by step he showed me that the *gift of God* is eternal life through Jesus Christ our Lord.

I saw the Gospel clearly that night. I was a wicked sinner—miserable, afraid to die—but I had not known how to be saved. I thought that being saved meant giving up sin, changing habits of life, quitting a lot of things I was doing. But that night God's minister showed me that *salvation is the GIFT OF GOD*, and that what I needed was to come to God, repenting of my sins, and accept His gift of salvation through faith in Jesus Christ, His Son.

Thank God, salvation cannot be *bought*—for then only the *rich* would be saved and the poor would have to spend eternity in hell! Salvation cannot be *earned*—for many would not be able to do enough to earn it. Salvation cannot be obtained any way except *God's way*. It is the *gift* of God and it has no connection with merit, good conduct, or right living. It is also completely apart from church membership, baptism, religious ceremonies, doctrines, or activities. It is God's gift to all who will receive it!

Saul of Tarsus was an intensely "religious" man before he became a Christian. In Philippians 3:4-6 he testified, ". . . If any other man thinketh that he hath whereof he might trust *in the flesh,* I more: Circumcised the eighth day, of the stock of Israel, of the tribe of Benjamin, *an Hebrew of the Hebrews;* as touching the law, *a Pharisee;* concerning zeal, persecuting the Church; *touching the righteousness which is in the law, blameless."* He followed the strictest order of the religion of the Jews, as he testified when he stood before King Agrippa (Acts 26:5). Yes, this man had *much* of which he could boast in the flesh and in the practice of "religion," but when Saul of Tarsus met the Lord Jesus Christ on the road to Damascus he became a new creation, a new man.

From that day forward, what things were gain to him from the standpoint of the flesh he counted loss for Christ, "for the excellency of the knowledge of Christ Jesus" (Phil. 3:7, 8), and immediately he began preaching Christ, the Son of God. You will find the moving, heart-warming account in Acts chapter 9.

Now let us look at some of the words penned by Paul the Apostle after he met Jesus on the Damascus road:

To the Corinthians he wrote of *salvation* as God's *unspeakable gift:* "Thanks be unto God for His unspeakable gift" (II Cor. 9:15).

To the Ephesians he wrote of God's *love* as *unknowable:* ". . . to know the love of Christ, *which PASSETH knowledge,* that ye might be filled with all the fulness of God" (Eph. 3:19).

Also to the Ephesians he wrote of the riches of Christ as *unsearchable:* "Unto me, who am less than the least of all saints, is this grace given, that I should preach among the Gentiles *the unsearchable riches of Christ*" (Eph. 3:8).

The missionary journeys of the Apostle Paul can be traced, but he declares that the ways of God are *untrackable:* "O the depth of the riches both of the wisdom and knowledge of God! How unsearchable are His judgments, *and His ways past finding out!*" (Rom. 11:33).

Paul, who had a "thorn in the flesh" and to whom God promised, "My grace is sufficient for thee" (II Cor. 12:7-9) declares that the grace of God is *inexhaustible:* "God is able to make *ALL grace abound* toward you, that ye, always having *all sufficiency in ALL THINGS*, may abound to every good work" (II Cor. 9:8).

Paul declared that the peace of God is *unfathomable:* "The peace of God, *which passeth all understanding*, shall keep your hearts and minds through Christ Jesus" (Phil. 4:7).

The superlative of Christ's perfection is beyond all question and all doubt. Christ the Son of God is the mightiest among the holy and the holiest among the mighty.

Christ Has Nothing For Sale

"Come unto me, all ye that labour and are heavy laden, and I will give you rest. Take my

yoke upon you, and learn of me; for I am meek
and lowly in heart: and ye shall find rest unto
your souls.   For my yoke is easy, and my burden
is light" (Matt. 11:28-30).

Thanks be unto God, *Jesus GIVES rest!* His
rest cannot be purchased, money cannot buy it.
It is free to all who come to Him through faith
in His finished work.

Jesus gives rest from a guilty conscience, having
"put away sin by the sacrifice of Himself" (Heb.
9:26).   He gives rest to the individual who exercises faith in His one sacrifice which satisfied God
—once, for all, forever.

Jesus gives rest from the fear of judgment, for
there is *"no condemnation* to them which are in
Christ Jesus" (Rom. 8:1).

Jesus gives rest from the fear of death, for by
Him death has been stripped of its power and
authority (Heb. 2:14).   He now holds the keys of
death and hell (Rev. 1:18) and He gives rest to all
who believe.

Jesus gives rest from *anxiety.* We are instructed
to "be careful for nothing; but in every thing by
prayer and supplication with thanksgiving let your
requests be made known unto God" (Phil. 4:6).

Jesus gives rest from the evil of unbelief, "for
we which have *believed* do enter into rest . . ."
(Heb. 4:3).

Jesus gives rest from defeat as we surrender to
Him and live in His presence, "because we have

sought the Lord our God, we have sought Him, and He hath given us rest on every side . . ." (II Chron. 14:7).

We are *safe* when we are resting in the finished work of Jesus.

We are *sure* when we are responding to His Word.

We are happy and fruitful, free from anxiety, when we are resting in His will.

Why are these things true? *Because Jesus is unchanging.* He is the same—"yesterday, and to day, and for ever" (Heb. 13:8).

The LOVE of Jesus is the same, it never changes. His Word declares, ". . . Yea, I have loved thee with an everlasting love . . ." (Jer. 31:3).

The POWER of Jesus is enduring, always the same: ". . . He hath said, I will never leave thee, nor forsake thee" (Heb. 13:5).

The MINISTRY of Jesus on our behalf is always the same. Seated at the right hand of God, He ever lives to make intercession for us (Heb. 7:25).

The PROMISES of Jesus are sure: "For all the promises of God in Him are yea, and in Him Amen, unto the glory of God by us" (II Cor. 1:20).

No wonder Paul cried out, *"Thanks be unto God for His UNSPEAKABLE GIFT!"*

God the Father Provided the Gift

Many wonderful, soul-stirring songs have been written about Jesus. As children most of us learned to sing "Jesus Loves Me"—and He does love little children. Then after we began to study our Bibles and attend church and prayermeetings, we began to sing the little chorus, "Every Day With Jesus Is Sweeter Than the Day Before"—and this, too, is true. But we must remember that it was God the Father in the beginning who so loved us that He gave His only begotten Son that we might find every day with Him sweeter than the day before. Had it not been for God's great love wherewith He loved us He could never have given His "unspeakable gift":

"For God so loved the world, that He gave His only begotten Son, that whosoever believeth in Him should not perish, but have everlasting life. For God sent not His Son into the world to condemn the world; but that the world through Him might be saved" (John 3:16, 17).

God knew the world would hate His Son, but even so, "God commendeth His love toward us, in that, while we were yet sinners, Christ died for us" (Rom. 5:8). God set Him forth "to be a propitiation through faith in His blood, to declare His righteousness for the remission of sins that are past, through the forbearance of God . . . that He might be just, and the Justifier of him which believeth in Jesus" (Rom. 3:25, 26).

God sent His Son into the world to do what no one else could do. Even God's holy law could not do what Jesus did:

"For what the law could not do, in that it was weak through the flesh, God sending His own Son in the likeness of sinful flesh, and for sin, condemned sin in the flesh: that the righteousness of the law might be fulfilled in us, who walk not after the flesh, but after the Spirit" (Rom. 8:3, 4).

To make possible the "unspeakable gift" of salvation God "spared not His own Son, but delivered Him up for us all" (Rom. 8:32). I do not profess to understand it, it is entirely too wonderful for me, but I know it is true because God's Word declares it: God made Jesus to be sin *for me,* that I, through Him, might be made righteous in the sight of God! "For He (God) hath made Him (Jesus) to be sin for us, who knew no sin (Jesus knew no sin); that we might be made the righteousness of God in Him" (II Cor. 5:21).

God gave Jesus. Jesus gave His blood. His blood satisfied God concerning the sin-debt; therefore the sin-debt is paid in full and it cannot be paid again. The only way you and I could become possessors of eternal life is to receive the unspeakable gift of God—Jesus Christ, God's Son and our Saviour.

How Do We Come Into Possession
of the Gift of God?

"As many as received HIM, to them gave He power to become the sons of God, even to them that believe on His name: which were born, not of blood, nor of the will of the flesh, nor of the will of man, but of God" (John 1:12, 13).

Thus the Bible clearly tells us how to obtain eternal life. In the preceding verses we are told that Jesus was in the world, the world that was made by Him, but "the world knew Him not." He came unto His own people, the Jews, but His own "received Him not." BUT—to *as MANY as received Him,* Jew, Gentile, rich, poor, bond or free, *He gave the power* to become the children of God. We have all received gifts at some time in our lives—at Christmas time, on birthdays or some other special occasion, so we all know what it means to receive something. Now what are some of the things that enter into the giving and receiving of a gift?

First of all, there must be love to prompt the giving.

Then, there must be a gift to give.

There must also be someone who is able and willing to give the gift.

There must then be someone to receive the gift.

God is love, God had a gift to give, God was able and willing to give the gift. Therefore the gift has been given, and all anyone in this world can do to become a recipient of salvation is to receive the Lord Jesus Christ by faith. Nothing can be bought, earned, or merited. The power to be born again cannot be worked up, prayed down, or worked for. It is the gift of God. As many as receive Jesus, to them God *gives* the power to become His children. The new birth is not of man's blood, it is not of man's will, it is not of the flesh. It is of God—of God's love, of God's will, of God's power, through faith in the shed blood of Jesus.

You see, man can no more "born" himself into the family of God than he can "born" himself into physical life. I owe my physical life to my mother's ability to give birth. I owe my eternal life (my spiritual life) to God's power which "borned" me into His family that night I heard and believed the Gospel in that little country church. As the minister talked with me, he took his New Testament and read John 3:16 to me. He asked me if I believed it. I told him I had always believed it. Then he said, "Yes, you have believed it with your head, you have believed it intellectually; but intellectual belief will not save you. You must believe from the *heart*. You must *trust and receive*."

He explained to me that if I would receive Jesus by faith, He would do for me what I could not do for myself—i. e., He would save me and make me a child of God. Forgetting my weakness and my sinfulness, I turned everything over to Jesus that night. With all the understanding and faith I had I believed and received Him into my heart—and He saved me! I was born into God's family by simply trusting Jesus, and there has not been one moment of doubt from that time until now. I KNOW that I am a child of God. I know WHOM I have believed.

John 3:18 is one of the greatest salvation verses in all the Bible. It clearly tells us who is saved—and why; and then just as clearly tells us who is *not* saved—and why. Notice:

"He that believeth on Him is not condemned . . . ." The individual who believes on Jesus *IS NOT condemned* (present tense). Therefore believers are not condemned. We are free from condemnation NOW.

"He that BELIEVETH NOT is condemned ALREADY." Just as believers are now free from condemnation, *unbelievers* are *under* condemnation—not at some future date, it is not a matter of *"going to be"* condemned; they are *condemned already.* Why? "Because he *hath not believed* in the name of the only begotten Son of God." Did someone question the simplicity of salvation? There it is: Those who believe on Jesus are not under condemnation. Those who *do not* believe are *already* condemned, and the *reason* for their condemnation is their *unbelief!*

Verse 36 of that same chapter in John's Gospel makes the same statement in different words: "He that believeth on the Son *HATH* (now) *everlasting life:* and he that *believeth not* the Son shall not see life; but the wrath of God *ABIDETH* (now) *on him."*

Jesus declared: "Verily, verily, I say unto you, He that *heareth my Word,* and *believeth* on Him that sent me, *HATH* (right now) *everlasting life,* and shall not come into condemnation; *but IS PASSED* (present tense) *from death unto life"* (John 5:24).

In I John 5:9-13 we find these enlightening words: "If we receive the witness of men, the witness of God is greater: for this is the witness of God which He hath testified of His Son." (If we believe the newspapers, magazines, and radio commentators, if we accept their witness, then surely we can believe the witness of God as laid down in His Word.)

"He that believeth on the Son of God hath the witness in himself. He that believeth not God hath made Him a liar, because he believeth not the record that God gave of His Son." (If we believe, we have the witness of the Holy Spirit within. If we do not believe, we make God a liar; that is, we declare that we do not believe what He says in His Word.)

"And this is the record, that God hath given to us eternal life, and this life is in His Son. He that hath the Son hath life (*now*), and he that hath not the Son of God hath not life. These things have I written unto you that believe on the name of the Son of God, *that ye may KNOW that ye have eternal life,* and that ye may believe on the name of the Son of God."

We come into possession of eternal life by believing on Jesus and receiving Him. If we have Jesus we have eternal life. If we do not have Jesus we do not have life. The only way to have Jesus is to believe the record God gives in His Word concerning His love for sinners, His sending Jesus into the world to die for sinners, and the death of Jesus on the cross that we through Him might live. That is the message that saves.

Eternal Life Is Christ In You

". . . I am made a minister, according to the dispensation of God which is given to me for you, to fulfil the Word of God; even the mystery which hath been hid from ages and from generations, but now is made manifest to His saints: to whom God would make known what is the riches of the glory of this mystery among the Gentiles—which is *CHRIST IN YOU, the hope of glory"* (Col. 1:25-27).

The Apostle Paul was God's minister to the Gentiles. He was the minister to the New Testament Church and to him God gave fourteen of the New Testament epistles. It was also to Paul that God revealed the "mystery" which had been hidden from all eternity, the mystery of the Church which is "Christ in you"—the only hope of any man entering glory!

In Colossians 3:1-4 Paul enlarges on the passage we have just quoted: "If ye then be risen with Christ, seek those things which are above, where

Christ sitteth on the right hand of God. Set your affection on things above, not on things on the earth. For ye are dead, and your life is hid with Christ in God. When Christ, who is our life, shall appear, then shall ye also appear with Him in glory."

Many people think of eternal life in terms of *length of years*, unending life; but that is only one phase of this great subject. It is not only *believers* who have unending life. Every *unsaved* person will live on after death. The difference is that unbelievers will live in torment, fear, pain, and misery in an eternal hell! They will know length of years, yes, but those years will extend through all eternity. The devil, the beast, the false prophet, and all the wicked will be cast into hell, "and the smoke of their torment ascendeth up for ever and ever: and they have no rest day nor night . . ." (Rev. 14:11; 19:20; 20:10).

So we see that *eternal life* is more than length of years, it is more than eternal existence. Eternal life is the life of Christ in the believer, for *He IS eternal life!* To have Christ is to have eternal life — *now*.

How Do We Know
That We Have Eternal Life?

There are three ways by which we can know that we possess eternal life:

1. The Word of God declares it.

The Word of God is truth (John 17:17). The

Word of God is forever settled in heaven (Psalm 119:89). Therefore we can safely depend on what God says in His Word, whether or not we "feel" saved. God promises that if we do what He requires us to do He will save us—and God cannot lie (Tit. 1:2). In Hebrews 6:17-20 we read:

"Wherein God, willing more abundantly to shew unto the heirs of promise the immutability of His counsel, *confirmed it by an oath: that by two immutable things, in which it was IMPOSSIBLE for God to lie, we might have a strong consolation,* who have fled for refuge to lay hold upon the hope set before us, which hope we have *as an anchor of the soul, both sure and stedfast,* and which entereth into that within the veil; whither the Forerunner is for us entered, even Jesus, made an High Priest for ever after the order of Melchisedec."

Who could ask for more assurance? Surely we can rely on the infallibility of God's Word! Now *where* does He tell us in His Word that believers have eternal life?

John 1:12, 13: "As many as *received Him,* to them gave He power to become the sons of God, even to them that believe on His name: which were born . . . of God." This passage from God's unalterable Word tells me that if I *receive Jesus,* the power of God will "born" me into the family of heaven. *I did* receive Jesus that night when the minister read John 3:16 to me, and God saved me as He promised He would.

John 3:18: "He that believeth on Him (Jesus) *is not condemned . . . .*" I know that I can safely believe what God promises. I believed on Jesus, therefore I am free from condemnation.

John 3:36: "He that believeth on the Son *HATH everlasting life . . . .*" I have believed on the Son of God, *therefore I HAVE* (right now) *everlasting life.* I know this because God's Word tells me so.

John 5:24: "Verily, verily, I say unto you, He that heareth my Word, and believeth on Him that sent me, hath everlasting life, and shall not come into condemnation; *but IS PASSED from death unto life.*" I heard the Word, I believed on God who sent Jesus to die for my sins, therefore I have everlasting life and I will *never* come into condemnation. I have already passed from death unto life!

2. *The Holy Spirit witnesses in the believer's heart.*

"Verily, verily, I say unto thee, Except a man be born again, he cannot see the kingdom of God. . . . Except a man be born of water and of the Spirit, he cannot enter into the kingdom of God. That which is born of the flesh is flesh; and that which is born of the Spirit is spirit" (John 3:3, 5, 6).

Except a man be born again he is not saved. There is no such thing as salvation apart from the new birth. However, it is the *spirit* of man that is born from above. That which is born of the flesh is flesh and always *will be* flesh.

When a person is born again, the Holy Spirit takes up His abode in that person's heart—and *"if any man HAVE NOT the Spirit of Christ, he is none of His"* (Rom. 8:9). Then, as the Holy Spirit abides in the inner man, He leads the believer "in the paths of righteousness for His name's sake" (Psalm 23:3). "As many as are led by the Spirit of God, they are the sons of God" (Rom. 8:14), and you may rest assured that the Spirit will lead Christians to do those things which will bring honor and glory to God.

The Holy Spirit within the heart of the believer also *assures* the believer that he is a child of God. "The Spirit Himself beareth witness with our spirit, that we are the children of God" (Rom. 8:16). And what is meant by "the witness of the Spirit"? It means that the Spirit in your heart assures you that sins are forgiven—assurance that comes not in an audible voice, but in peace and tranquility of soul and mind. The witness of the Spirit takes away the fear of death, it removes the fear of judgment, and makes the believer unafraid to meet God.

In God's love letter to His "little children" we read, "These things write we unto you, *that your joy may be full*" (I John 1:4). How could anyone possibly be happy and have full joy unless he has perfect assurance that he is *saved?* But we do have that assurance! In I John 3, the last part of verse 24, we read: *"Hereby we KNOW that He abideth in us, by the Spirit which He hath given us."* Again, in I John 4:13 we find this assurance: *"Hereby we KNOW that we dwell in Him, and He in us, because He hath given us of HIS SPIRIT."* So by the witness of the Holy Spirit in our hearts, we know that we are born again and sure for heaven!

The Holy Spirit "borns" us into God's family, leads us in paths of righteousness, assures us that we are children of God—but He does more: A person who possesses the Holy Spirit will most assuredly bear at least a portion of the *fruit* of the Spirit:

"The fruit of the Spirit is love, joy, peace, long-suffering, gentleness, goodness, faith, meekness, temperance: against such there is no law" (Gal. 5:22,23). Certainly one who is born again will display the fruit of love! He will love God, and he will love the "brethren." John the Beloved declares, *"We KNOW that we have passed from death unto life, because we love the brethren . . ."* (I John 3:14).

Before I was saved I had neither desire nor time for the house of God and the people of God; but immediately after I was saved I longed to be in the house of God, I longed for fellowship with the children of God. Before I was saved I frequented nightclubs, dancehalls, and beer parlors; but since I have been a child of God I have had no desire for such places—nor would I feel comfortable in them. Born again people are new creations. We love new things. We practice new habits of life, we have new friends. We even speak a new language and sing a new song. Whereas while we lived in sin we followed the broad way "that leadeth to destruction," after we are saved the Holy Spirit leads us in new paths, in the way "which leadeth unto life" (Matt. 7:13, 14).

If you do not have the witness of the Spirit in your heart, bow your head and talk to God about it. Ask Him in the name of Jesus to save you by His grace and give you the witness of the Spirit in your heart. I assure you on the authority of His Word that He will save you and will give you the assurance of your salvation. Notice I did not say that you will have a great emotional experience. I did not say that you will laugh, or cry, or clap your hands. You might do either or all of those things. If you do, it will be perfectly all right— but it will add nothing to your salvation. Believe on the Lord Jèsus Christ and God will "born" you into His family through the incorruptible seed by the power of the Holy Spirit. As many as receive Jesus, to them God gives the power to become the children of God.

3. *The believer's heart is free from condemnation.*
"If our heart condemn us, God is greater than

our heart, and knoweth all things. Beloved, if our heart condemn us not, then have we confidence toward God" (I John 3:20, 21).

"Man looketh on the outward appearance, but the Lord looketh on the heart" (I Sam. 16:7).

God deals with the heart and the Bible tells us why: "Keep thy heart with all diligence, *for out of it are the issues of life*" (Prov. 4:23). The heart is the *seat* of life, and out of it are the *issues* of life. If the heart is bad, everything about us is bad. But when we are saved, God puts a new heart within us and we are righteous in His sight. "A *new heart* also will I give you, and a *new spirit* will I put within you . . ." (Ezek. 36:26).

When we are born again we are new creations in Christ. "Old things are passed away; behold, all things are become new" (II Cor. 5:17). We have new life *because Christ IS our life:*

"If ye then be risen with Christ, seek those things which are above, where Christ sitteth on the right hand of God. Set your affection on things above, not on things on the earth. For ye are dead, and your life is hid with Christ in God. When Christ, who is our life, shall appear, then shall ye also appear with Him in glory" (Col. 3:1-4).

The moment we are saved we become partakers of divine nature—that is, *divine nature dwells within,* in the Person of the Holy Spirit. The entire life of a believer is changed instantaneously when he believes unto salvation. I do not mean that he automatically lays off all doubtful things at that moment. We *grow* in grace, but God does not redeem us by degrees. We are perfectly redeemed the moment we believe, because God puts within us a new heart from which the issues of life proceed, and the life that proceeds from the new heart is the life of Christ. As Paul expresses it in Galatians 2:20, "I am crucified with Christ: nevertheless I live; *yet not I, but Christ liveth in me:* and the life which I now live in the flesh I live by the faith of the Son of God, who loved me, and gave Himself for me!"

In Psalm 24:3, 4 we read, "Who shall ascend into the hill of the LORD? or who shall stand in His holy place? *He that hath clean hands, and A PURE HEART . . . .*" Only the pure in heart can enter the city of God. In Matthew 5:8 Jesus declares, "Blessed are the pure in heart, for they shall see God."

When God saves a sinner, He does not simply "overhaul" or repair the heart. He literally puts a *new* heart within the bosom of that sinner when he is saved. I am not speaking of removing the muscle of flesh which is the physical heart, for flesh is only flesh. The life of the flesh is in the blood, and Jesus gave His blood to purchase the Church (Acts 20:28). Therefore the blood of Jesus, applied to the heart by faith, gives the believer a new heart, a *pure* heart, and the "pure in heart" shall see God.

In Acts 8:26-39 we find a beautiful picture of salvation by grace through faith in the finished work of the Lord Jesus Christ. Philip was in Samaria where he was conducting a very successful revival. But the angel of the Lord spoke to him and said, "Arise, and go toward the south unto the way that goeth down from Jerusalem unto Gaza, which is desert."

Obedient to the Lord's direction, Philip started toward Gaza. As he traveled he met an Ethiopian eunuch, a man of great authority under Candace, queen of Ethiopia. The eunuch was returning from Jerusalem where he had gone to worship, and as he journeyed he was reading the scroll of Isaiah.

The Holy Spirit instructed Philip to go and join the eunuch, and as Philip drew near the eunuch's chariot he heard the man reading from Isaiah. Philip asked him, "Understandest thou what thou readest?" The eunuch replied, "How can I, except some man should guide me?" And he invited Philip to ride with him and explain the Scriptures.

So Philip took the scroll and read from Isaiah, chapter 53: "He was led as a sheep to the slaughter; and like a lamb dumb before his shearer, so opened He not His mouth. In His humiliation His judgment was taken away: and who shall declare His generation? for His life is taken from the earth.''

The eunuch then asked Philip of whom this passage was speaking, and Philip "began at the same Scripture, *and preached unto him JESUS.*" As they continued on their way, they came to a body of water and the eunuch asked, "What doth hinder me to be baptized?" Now here is the verse I want you to literally appropriate, assimilate, and digest:

"Philip said, *If thou believest with all thine HEART, thou mayest.*" The eunuch answered, *"I BELIEVE that Jesus Christ is the Son of God!"* Then Philip commanded the chariot to stand still and they went down into the water where he baptized the eunuch. "And when they were come up out of the water, the Spirit of the Lord caught away Philip, that the eunuch saw him no more: and he went on his way rejoicing!"

Now here is the message I would like for you to get from this passage: The Ethiopian eunuch had traveled all the way from his own country to Jerusalem for the purpose of worshipping God. He had gone through all the ceremonies of the temple, he had observed the rituals in the religion of the Jews, but he was returning home with the same hungry heart, still seeking satisfaction for his soul. After Philip preached Jesus and the eunuch asked to be baptized, Philip said, *"If thou believest with all thine HEART,* thou mayest." Believe what? What was it the eunuch must believe with all of his heart? He answered Philip, "I believe that *Jesus Christ is the Son of God"*— and Philip baptized him. Salvation is an affair of the *heart,* beloved. Jesus (in the Person of the Holy Spirit) abides in the heart of every born again believer, and *the Holy Spirit in our heart* assures us that Jesus is there. If your heart gives no such assurance, *Jesus is NOT there!*

Acts 16:14, 15 gives another account of heart salvation. Paul and Silas went into Europe to preach the Gospel, and a woman named Lydia heard Paul preach. Lydia was a devout woman, she worshipped God, following Him with all the light she had up to that time. Paul's message was always *Christ—the Son of God,* crucified, risen, ascended, coming again. He testified that he was determined not to know anything "save Jesus Christ, and Him crucified" (I Cor. 2:2). So whatever his message the night Lydia heard him, it was *"Christ crucified."* As this woman listened, *the Lord opened her HEART* and she believed Paul's message. We are not told that God opened her *mind.* This was not an intellectual belief. The Apostle Paul was a scholar, one of the best educated men of his day, and Lydia was a seller of purple, a woman who dealt with the elite of society. Therefore Paul could have *preached* an "intellectual" sermon and Lydia could have *believed* intellectually. But it was her *heart* that the Lord opened, and it was *with her heart* that she believed unto salvation.

Now let us look at another individual, one who did *not* believe with the heart, Simon the sorcerer, whose record is found in Acts 8:9-25. Simon lived in the city of Samaria, where he practiced his sorceries and held great power over the people; but when Philip came into the city preaching the Gospel, many people believed his message and were baptized.

Then the church at Jerusalem sent Peter and John to Samaria to help Philip, and as Simon the sorcerer watched these men, beholding the miracles and wonders done in the name of Jesus, he wondered, he was amazed. He saw Peter and John lay their hands on those who believed, and they received the Holy Ghost. So he approached the apostles and said, "Give me also this power, that on whomsoever I lay hands, he may receive the Holy Ghost" – and he offered them money.

Peter said to him, *"Thy money perish with thee, because thou hast thought that the gift of God may be purchased with money. Thou hast neither part nor lot in this matter: for thy HEART is not right in the sight of God!* Repent therefore of this thy wickedness, and pray God, if perhaps *the thought of thine HEART* may be forgiven thee. For I perceive that thou art in the gall of bitterness, and in the bond of iniquity."

You will notice in verse 13 of this passage, when Simon saw the people believing through Philip's preaching, "Simon himself believed also" and was baptized along with the others—but *what* did he believe? He believed that Philip wrought miracles. He believed that Jesus was raised from the dead as Philip declared. These things were in complete harmony with his own claims of power for he, too, claimed to work miracles and claimed to be from God. It was not impossible for him to believe the declarations Philip made and accept the miracles he saw performed, *but he was not concerned about the redemption of his soul.*

Simon sought monetary gain, and when he saw the extraordinary results of Peter and John laying hands on the Samaritans he knew that if he could only possess such power he could greatly increase his fortune. So he offered money in return for the gift of being able to bestow the Holy Spirit upon others! This is proof enough that he was not a born again Christian, for if he had been saved by grace he would have known that the third Person of the Godhead is not for sale and the power of God can be obtained only through faith in the shed blood of the Lord Jesus Christ.

But notice Peter said to him, *"Thy HEART is not right* in the sight of God." Simon had not heard Philip's message with his heart. He had heard only with his mind, an intellectual understanding, and he saw what he thought was an opportunity to add another avenue to his income. Peter advised him to (1) repent, and (2) pray for forgiveness. There is no indication that Simon was ever saved. Instead of repenting and praying, he asked Peter and John to pray for him, "that none of these things which ye have spoken come upon me." He wanted them to pray for him—not because he had a penitent *heart*, but because he was thinking of the punishment that might come upon him according to their observations!

It is possible for a person to "reform" under his own strength of will, but it is not possible for him to *redeem* himself. Only the blood of Jesus redeems, and only through His blood can we have eternal life. Jesus said, "Ye shall know them by their fruits" (Matt. 7:16). Then in Luke 6:43-45 He explained:

"For a good tree bringeth not forth corrupt fruit; neither doth a corrupt tree bring forth good fruit. For every tree is known by his own fruit. For of thorns men do not gather figs, nor of a bramble bush gather they grapes. A good man out of *the good treasure of his HEART* bringeth forth that which is *good;* and an evil man out of *the EVIL treasure of his HEART* bringeth forth that which is *evil:* for *of the abundance of the HEART his mouth speaketh!*"

God forbid that I should judge my fellowman; but *the fruit declares the nature of the tree.* Men live bad lives because they have a bad heart. That is not judging, it is simply inspecting fruit. Men and women who gamble, drink, curse, lie, cheat, steal, live in sin, lust, and ungodliness *simply are not saved.* A born again person may stumble and fall, yes, but he will not stay down. He will have the same spirit of repentance Peter had the night he denied his Lord and then met the eyes of Jesus from across the courtyard as the Lord turned and looked at him! One look from Jesus broke the big fisherman's heart, and he went out and wept bitterly. From then until the day he died he was a dedicated, stalwart servant of the Lord Jesus Christ. It is possible for a true believer to backslide, but he will not stay in that condition. He will return to Christ, as Peter did, and seek restored fellowship.

Beloved, *do YOU have HEART salvation?* Or do you have "religion"? Unless you have been *born* of God, unless your heart assures you that you are prepared to *meet* God, then I warn you that you are not saved. No, I am not judging, I am simply comparing Scripture with Scripture and putting your experience in the balance. Nothing is further removed from the Scriptures than the idea that Christians must wait until after death to find out whether or not they are really saved! What a tragedy it would be to depart this life thinking (or hoping) you are saved, only to discover that you are *not* saved and must spend eternity in hell. The Scriptures teach no such doctrine.

It is as impossible to have spiritual life and not know it, as it is impossible to have physical life and not know it. When a baby is born into this world, people find it out. The baby testifies by crying, by moving. When one is born into the kingdom of God a new life begins. The born again individual knows it, and the people around that individual find it out! It will be announced in many ways. So if you do not know that you are a child of God as surely as you know you are living physically, then I would certainly hate to die with your brand of religion!

I know I am a child of God. That is not boasting, it is simply taking God at His Word. The Word of God tells me that I am saved, and God cannot lie. Oh, yes—my "feelings" change. There are days when great peace floods my soul. There are other days when I have unusual joy, and still other days when I have heavy burdens upon me which depress me and weigh me down. But I am just as saved on those days as I am on the days when I have unusual peace, or joy. Thanks be unto God, salvation does not depend on "thrills" or "chills," but on *"Thus saith the Lord."* No one will ever drop into hell by standing on the Word of God! I may not be all that I should be, I may not be all that I want to be, I may not have done everything just as it should have been done; but I know beyond all doubt that if I should die within the next sixty seconds I am ready to meet God. *Are YOU?*

We are saved by God's grace, God's grace becomes ours by faith. Faith becomes ours by hearing the Word. The Word of God is the incorruptible seed that brings the new birth. If you are not saved, I beg you to read these verses, obey them, and then call on God in the name of Jesus. He will save you—and you will know it!

Ephesians 2:8-10: "For by grace are ye saved *through faith;* and that not of yourselves: it is the gift of God: not of works, lest any man should boast. For we are His workmanship, created in Christ Jesus unto good works, which God hath before ordained that we should walk in them."

Romans 10:17: "So then faith cometh by hearing, and hearing by the Word of God."

I Peter 1:23: "Being born again, not of corruptible seed, but of incorruptible, *by the Word of God, which liveth and abideth for ever.*"

James 1:18, 21: "Of His own will begat He us *with the Word of truth,* that we should be a kind of firstfruits of His creatures. . . . Wherefore lay apart all filthiness and superfluity of naughtiness, and *receive with meekness the engrafted Word, which is able to save your souls.*"

Romans 10:9, 10: "If thou shalt confess with thy mouth the Lord Jesus, and shalt *believe in thine heart* that God hath raised Him from the dead, *thou shalt be saved.* For *with the heart man believeth* unto righteousness; and with the mouth confession is made unto salvation."

DOES SALVATION PRODUCE FEELINGS?

Does Salvation Produce Feelings ?

"I am not ashamed of the Gospel of Christ: for it is the power of God unto *salvation* to every one that believeth; to the Jew first, and also to the Greek" (Rom. 1:16).

". . . *Salvation* is of the Lord" (Jonah 2:9).

"*Salvation* belongeth unto the Lord . . ." (Psalm 3:8).

". . . And the Lord added to the Church daily such as (were being) *saved*" (Acts 2:47).

". . . Sirs, what must I do to be *saved?* . . . Believe on the Lord Jesus Christ, and thou shalt be *saved,* and thy house" (Acts 16:30, 31).

Notice in all of the verses the words "salvation" or "saved" appear, but *not once* is "religion" used. In fact, the term "religion" is used in Scripture only once with reference to salvation— in James 1:27 where we read of "*pure religion* and undefiled." Of course, "pure religion" is salvation. There are many "religions," but there is only one Saviour, one salvation, one Way to heaven. The question asked in the title of this message is not "Does *religion* produce feelings?" but "Does *salvation* produce feelings?" This is a Bible question, and the only place to find the answer to Bible

111

questions is in the Bible. Evangelists, ministers, and teachers would not agree on whether or not salvation produces feelings, therefore we will go to the Word of God to find the answer:

First of all, we might ask the following questions: *What IS salvation?* How do we *obtain* salvation? How do we know that we *have* salvation? How do we *keep* salvation? And if salvation does produce "feelings," what kind of feeling does it produce? During the course of our study in this message we will answer these questions from the Word of God.

There is much false doctrine being taught and preached by the false teachers and false preachers who are abroad in the land today, and this has brought about much confusion among church people concerning "religion" and salvation. Instead of preaching "Thus saith the Lord," too many preachers are preaching man-made doctrine, dogma, and tradition. Jesus said, *"Ye shall know the TRUTH, and the truth shall make you FREE"* (John 8:32). And the Apostle Paul adds, under inspiration of the Holy Spirit, *"Let GOD be true, but every man a liar!"* (Rom. 3:4). Truth does not bring confusion. It brings liberty, freedom, peace, and understanding.

What is salvation? Salvation is *Christ in the believer* (Col. 1:27). Salvation is "being born again, not of corruptible seed, but of incorruptible, by the Word of God, which liveth and abideth for ever" (I Pet. 1:23). Joining the local church is not salvation. Living a clean upright moral life is not salvation. Being "religious" is not salvation. A person may join a church, be baptized in water, give ten percent of his income, and live daily above reproach—but that does not mean that he is saved. "Except a man be *born again* (born from above), *he cannot see the kingdom of God*" (John 3:3).

The beginning of salvation is hearing God's Word: "Verily, verily, I say unto you, He that heareth my Word, and believeth on Him that sent me, hath everlasting life, and shall not come into condemnation; but is passed from death into life" (John 5:24). "Of His own will begat He us with the Word of Truth, that we should be a kind of firstfruits of His creatures. . . . Wherefore lay apart all filthiness and superfluity of naughtiness, and *receive with meekness* **THE ENGRAFTED WORD**, *which is able to save your souls*" (James 1:18, 21).

In John 5:24 Jesus clearly tells us that two things are necessary in order to become a possessor of salvation: (1) We must hear the Word of God. (2) We must believe on God who sent Jesus. There are many reasons why people join a church. They join for business reasons, for social reasons, because they think it is the "proper" thing to do, and for many other reasons; but there is only one reason why a person confesses his sins and submits heart and soul to God: That reason is because he hears the Word of God, realizes his lost condition, recognizes the solemn fact that the wages of sin is death—and then discovers the glorious truth that "the gift of God is eternal life through Jesus Christ our Lord" (Rom. 6:23).

The Word of God is the only place where we can learn that we are saved by grace—God's unearned, unmerited, undeserved favor. The Word of God tells us that God so loved us that He "commendeth His love toward us, in that, while we were yet sinners, Christ died for us" (Rom. 5:8). When we hear the Word, faith is born in the heart, and faith brings saving grace:

"For *by grace are ye saved through faith;* and that not of yourselves: *it is the GIFT OF GOD*" (Eph. 2:8). Grace does the saving, and saving grace becomes ours when we exercise faith in God through the finished work of Christ. Grace saves us, faith appropriates grace, and "faith cometh by hearing, and hearing by the Word of God" (Rom. 10:17). So the only way to come into possession of saving faith is to hear the Word of God. We hear and believe the Word, believing the Word brings faith, faith brings grace, and grace saves us.

When we hear the Word of God, *what do we hear?* John 3:16 tells us, "God so loved the world, that He gave His only begotten Son, that whosoever believeth in Him should not perish, but have everlasting life."

In John 6:37 the Word of God says, "Him that

cometh to me I will in no wise cast out."

Matthew 11:28 invites, "Come unto me, all ye that labour and are heavy laden, and I will give you rest."

Romans 10:13, 14 tells us, "Whosoever shall call upon the name of the Lord shall be saved. How then shall they call on Him in whom they have not believed? and how shall they believe in Him of whom they have not heard? and how shall they hear without a preacher?"

So according to the Word of God, He loved us, He gave His Son to die for us, His Son came into the world and invited "whosoever will," "Come unto me. . . . I will in no wise cast you out." Today the preacher preaches the Word of God, the sinner hears the Word, and through hearing the Word he learns of the love God has for poor, lost souls. The sinner believes the Word, believing God's Word brings faith. Faith exercised in God brings grace, and grace saves. It is only when the sinner *hears* and *believes* that he can call in faith, and when he calls upon God in faith, God saves him for Christ's sake (Eph. 4:32).

There are hundreds of religions and cults on earth today, and they can all be summarized under one or the other of two headings:

(1) Love.

(2) Fear.

But when the many, many religions of the world have been catalogued under their proper classification, you will find *only ONE* (Christianity) under the heading of "Love." All others must be listed under *"FEAR."* Only Christianity comes by and through and because of love—*GOD'S love. God IS love* (I John 4:8). We love Him because He first loved us (I John 4:19), and we who are born again serve God *because we LOVE Him,* not because we are afraid of Him.

The *"religions"* of the world teach their people to serve, labor, and *give* because of fear. I have traveled extensively in foreign countries in the interest of missions. I have seen many religions in as many lands. I have observed that the thousands upon thousands of people who support these various religions attend services (or rituals) and give of their means because they are afraid *not* to attend services, they are afraid *not* to give. There is no love in their worship. On the contrary, they live in continual fear.

Proverbs 1:7 declares, "The *fear of the Lord* is the beginning of knowledge"—and it is true that believers fear God; but there is a vast difference between *fearing* God and being *afraid* of God. As children of God we seek His pleasure and His will, knowing that "whom the Lord loveth He chasteneth" (Heb. 12:6). But we are not *afraid* of Him because being justified by the blood of Jesus "we shall be saved from wrath through Him" (Rom. 5:9). I John 4:17, 18 explains, "Herein is our love made perfect, that we may have boldness in the day of judgment: because *as HE is, so are WE in this world.* There is no fear in love; but perfect love casteth out fear: because fear hath torment. He that feareth is not made perfect in love."

God cannot lie (Tit. 1:2; Heb. 6:18). Therefore we who are born again know that we are free from sin and Satan. We have perfect liberty, for "if the Son therefore shall make you free, ye shall be free indeed" (John 8:36).

We are saved, made righteous, given everlasting life through hearing, believing, and receiving the Word of God. No wonder the devil hates the Word of God as he does. No wonder that in these days of modernism and liberal preaching he is doing all in his power to discredit the Scriptures! With the new translations—and *revisions* of the new translations—which are being printed and distributed by the millions, many people are asking, "Which Bible is right?" The *Word of God* is right. Always has been, always will be. The Word of God is forever settled in heaven (Psalm 119:89), and the devil cannot get his wicked hands on it!

Personally, I accept the old-fashioned King James version of the Bible. I use other translations for study and reference, but when it comes to a final decision I always return to the King James. How could any sinner ever become a child of God if it were not for the Word of God? It is only through the Word that we learn the glorious truth that Jesus came to seek and to save the lost. It is only through the Word that anyone—yes, even you and I—can know of the love of God and the sacrifice Jesus made on Calvary that we might be saved. It is only through the Word that we find faith to appropriate God's saving grace through faith in the shed blood of Jesus.

Beloved, the devil cares not how many sermons a minister preaches, nor how sincerely he preaches, as long as he does not preach *the pure, unadulterated Word of God!* It is the preaching of the Gospel that the devil opposes, and the definition of the Gospel is clearly stated in I Corinthians 15:1-4:

"Moreover, brethren, I declare unto you the Gospel which I preached unto you, which also ye have received, and wherein ye stand. . . . For I delivered unto you first of all that which I also received, how that Christ died for our sins according to the Scriptures; and that He was buried, and that He rose again the third day according to the Scriptures."

Salvation the Gift of God

"For by grace are ye saved through faith; and that not of yourselves: it is the *gift* of God" (Eph. 2:8).

"For the wages of sin is death; but the *gift* of God is eternal life through Jesus Christ our Lord" (Rom. 6:23).

Does Salvation Produce Feelings?

"As many as received Him, to them *gave* He power to become the sons of God, even to them that believe on His name" (John 1:12).

Everything pertaining to salvation is *God's GIFT.* First of all, God has given His Word: "For the prophecy came not in old time by the will of man: but holy men of God spake as they were moved by the Holy Ghost" (II Pet. 1:21). Yes, the Word of God that enlightens, informs, and brings saving faith is the gift of God.

Then, God gives the power to become His child, the power to be born from above; and this power comes through the Gospel, "the power of God unto salvation" (Rom. 1:16). Power to become sons of God is not worked up, earned, or purchased. *It is the gift of God.* And *ONLY God* has the power to perform the miracle of the new birth. We cannot "born" ourselves into God's family. The new birth is not of man's blood, it is not of man's flesh, it is not of man's will. It is of God's power that we are born again (John 1:13; 3:3, 5).

Yes, salvation is as truly a birth as the natural birth is a real birth, and the spiritual birth occurs when the seed of the Word is planted in the heart of the sinner. The unbeliever who *refuses to hear* the Word of God closes the door of salvation in his own face, for the seed must come into the heart and bring forth life in order to produce the miracle of the new birth. But when one hears and

believes the Word of God, faith bursts forth into
life in that person's sinful heart and he is born
again by the power of God. The grace of God
brings salvation through faith which appropriates
God's grace unto salvation. The only possible way
to receive anything from God is by faith, and
without faith it is impossible to please Him (Heb.
11:6). Moreover, *whatsoever is NOT of faith is SIN*
(Rom. 14:23).

Seven Steps of Saving Faith

Abraham is known as the father of the faithful.
"Abraham believed God, and it was counted unto
him for righteousness" (Rom. 4:3). The first eight
verses of Genesis chapter 12 clearly outline the
seven steps Abraham took that led to salvation
and to his becoming known as the father of the
faithful and friend of God:

"Now the Lord had said unto Abram, Get thee
out of thy country, and from thy kindred, and
from thy father's house, unto a land that I will
shew thee: and I will make of thee a great nation,
and I will bless thee, and make thy name great;
and thou shalt be a blessing. And I will bless
them that bless thee, and curse him that curseth
thee: and in thee shall all families of the earth
be blessed.

"So Abram departed, as the Lord had spoken
unto him; and Lot went with him: and Abram
was seventy and five years old when he departed

out of Haran. And Abram took Sarai his wife, and Lot his brother's son, and all their substance that they had gathered, and the souls that they had gotten in Haran; and they went forth to go into the land of Canaan; and into the land of Canaan they came.

"And Abram passed through the land unto the place of Sichem, unto the plain of Moreh. And the Canaanite was then in the land. And the Lord appeared unto Abram, and said, Unto thy seed will I give this land: and there builded he an altar unto the Lord, who appeared unto him. And he removed from thence unto a mountain on the east of Bethel, and pitched his tent, having Bethel on the west, and Hai on the east: and there he builded an altar unto the Lord, and called upon the name of the Lord" (Gen. 12:1-8).

1. The beginning of faith:—

God commanded Abraham, *"Get thee out of thy country,* and from thy kindred, and from thy father's house, *unto a land that I will shew thee."* God gave Abraham no road maps, He put no signs along the way. He simply gave His Word—*"I will show thee."* And Abraham believed God.

2. The call of faith:—

"Get thee out . . . from thy father's house." I do not doubt that Abraham was well situated with his father and his kinsmen in his own land. His future seemed secure, nothing lacking. Yet

121

in the midst of security and comfort came God's call of faith. "Get up and get out"—to a place unknown to Abraham, to a land as yet unnamed to him, and he would travel by a path uncharted, known only to God. But God said, "I will show you"—and Abraham was willing to follow where God led.

3. *The promise of faith:—*

The first three verses of Genesis chapter 12 contain the four *"I will's"* of God's promise to Abraham:

"I will shew thee. . . .

"I will make of thee a great nation. . . .

"I will bless thee, and make thy name great. . . .

"I will bless them that bless thee, and curse him that curseth thee. . . ."

4. *The blessing of faith:—*

"I will bless thee. . . . I will bless them that bless thee. . . . In thee shall all families of the earth be blessed." All who are in the faith are blessed of God, and born again Christians are a blessing to those with whom they come in contact.

5. *The obedience of faith:—*

"So Abram departed, as the Lord had spoken unto him." Hebrews 11:8 tells us, *"By faith* Abraham, when he was called to go out into a place which he should after receive for an inheritance, *obeyed;* and *he went out, not knowing whither he went.''* Abraham believed what God said and he obeyed without question, journeying as his steps were ordered by the Lord, looking "for a city which hath foundations, whose builder and maker is God" (Heb. 11:10).

6. *The concern of faith:—*

God told only Abraham to get up and get out of his country, and Abraham obeyed without question. But he was concerned about his family. The Bible teaches that a man who does not provide for those of his own house "hath denied the faith, and is worse than an infidel" (I Tim. 5:8). So Abraham took Sarah his wife, and Lot, his nephew, *"and all their substance that they had gathered, and the souls that they had gotten in Haran.''* He left nothing behind. When God called him, he obeyed with all that he had.

7. *The enemy of faith—and how to conquer it:—*

When Abraham and his family came into the land of Canaan *"the Canaanite was then in the land.''* God did not clear the way before Abraham arrived in the promised land. But notice: *"The Lord appeared unto Abram,* and said, Unto thy seed will I give this land." God always appears just when we need Him most, and we are more than conquerors through Him (Rom. 8:37). We have victory guaranteed when we have Jesus: "There hath no temptation taken you but such as is common to man: but God is faithful, who

123

will not suffer you to be tempted above that ye are able; but will with the temptation also make a way to escape, that ye may be able to bear it" (I Cor. 10:13).

Yes, the enemy was in the land when Abraham arrived there, but God promised, *"Unto thy seed will I GIVE this land"* — and Abraham believed God. And then — Abraham *"builded an altar unto the Lord, and called upon the name of the Lord."* Abraham heard God's command, he believed and obeyed what he heard. By faith he left his country and followed where God led. He built an altar, and at that altar, in prayer, he met the enemy of faith.

Jesus promised, "Ask, and it shall be given you; seek, and ye shall find; knock, and it shall be opened unto you" (Matt. 7:7).

James tells us, ". . . ye have not, because ye ask not. Ye ask, and receive not, because ye ask amiss, that ye may consume it upon your lusts" (James 4:2, 3).

But — "what saith the Scripture? *ABRAHAM BELIEVED GOD, and it was counted unto him for righteousness!"* (Rom. 4:3).

Saved Persons Are New Creatures

We are saved by being born again through the power of God, through the incorruptible seed — the Word of God; and when we are born again we become new creations:

Does Salvation Produce Feelings?

"Therefore if any man be in Christ, he is a new creature: old things are passed away; behold, all things are become new" (II Cor. 5:17).

The born again believer will live right—not in order to *be* saved, but because he *is* saved and God has given him a new heart (Ezek. 36:26). Without a new heart it would be impossible to live a new life. Without a new heart it would be impossible to live righteously. That is why many church members cannot live as they should. They "join" a church, they go through the ritual of water baptism, they attend services, they give of their financial means to support the "program"; but six days a week they live the same life they lived before they joined the church. The sad truth is that they have never been born again, they have never received a new heart, they are not partakers of divine nature, and they are trying to do in the flesh what can be done *only IN CHRIST*. They are not children of God, they are just "church members."

You see, although redemption is complete the very moment we believe on Jesus, *salvation does MORE than redeem us*. Day by day it saves us from the slavery and power of sin as we trust Jesus and feed upon His Word.

So our salvation delivers us from the penalty and condemnation of sin (Rom. 8:1), and keeps us day by day from the power of sin as we abide in Christ and look to Him who lives in our heart.

And in the future—it could be within the next hour, day, or week—Jesus will save every born again believer from the very presence of sin! True believers wait for Him who will appear from heaven and take us where He is (Phil. 3:20; John 14:1-3).

The Christ who saves us also keeps us for Himself (I Pet. 1:5); and He will return the second time to receive us unto Himself. "So Christ was once offered to bear the sins of many; *and unto them that LOOK for Him* shall He appear the second time without sin unto salvation" (Heb. 9:28).

Salvation and Feelings

There is much confusion on the subject of salvation and feelings. Many of God's dear people do not receive the Word of God at face value. They do not accept Bible facts and stand firmly on God's Word. Regardless of what men may teach, if we would enjoy our Christian birthright we must stand upon "Thus saith the Lord."

The words "feel" and "feelings" are used very few times in the Bible, and they are not used *at all* in connection with salvation from sin. "Rest . . . peace . . . joy"—these are the words that describe salvation.

What is the *definition* of "feeling"? According to Webster, it is "one of the five senses of which the skin is the chief end organ, and of which sensations of touch and pressure are characteristics, specifically touch; a sensation or a perception;

126

bodily consciousness; any emotional state." So "feeling" is one of the five senses, the skin being the chief organ through which we *feel.* It is also *an emotional state.*

What does the Bible say about *salvation?* "That which is born of the flesh is flesh; and that which is born of the Spirit is spirit" (John 3:6). ". . . man looketh on the outward appearance, but the Lord looketh on the heart" (I Sam. 16:7). It is the heart and the spirit—not the skin—which God makes new. Therefore "feelings" *as such* have nothing to do with salvation, and salvation does not necessarily produce feelings. Rest? Yes. Peace? Yes. Quiet of spirit and soul? Yes. *But feelings?* Not necessarily.

Now lest someone lay this message aside and refuse to read further, I hasten to say that there is no such thing as salvation apart from assurance. All born again people *know* they are born again. We cannot be saved and not know it. But the assurance of salvation does not come merely because we "*feel*" saved. God deliver us from personal workers, counselors, ministers, evangelists, and teachers who deal with a seeking soul, and then at the climax of instruction ask that person, "Do you *feel* saved?" I have personally heard that question asked in the inquiry room. Never ask a seeking soul if he *feels* saved. We are not saved by "feelings," *we are saved by FAITH!*

Jesus said, "Come unto me, all ye that labour

and are heavy laden, and *I will give you REST*. Take my yoke upon you, and learn of me; for I am meek and lowly in heart: and *ye shall find REST unto your souls*" (Matt. 11:28, 29). There is no word here about "feelings." Jesus said, "I will give you REST"—and *what is rest?* Again we turn to the dictionary and find this definition of rest: ". . . quiet, tranquility, peace of mind or spirit." So Jesus said, "Come unto me—and I will give you rest. I will deliver you from fear, from the dread of meeting God in eternity. I will give you tranquility of spirit and soul. I will take away the anxiety that sin and unbelief produce."

Again, Jesus said, "Peace I leave with you, *MY peace* I give unto you: not as the world giveth, give I unto you. Let not your heart be troubled, neither let it be afraid" (John 14:27). Now what was Jesus saying here? "Come to me. Put your trust in me, and I will give you *peace*—not the kind of peace the world gives, but *MY peace*, peace of mind and heart."

Let us look at the definition of "peace": ". . . a pact, an agreement to end hostilities between those who have been at war or in a state of hostility; a state of tranquility or quiet; freedom from fears, agitating passions, moral conflict."

The day Adam disobeyed God and ate of the forbidden fruit, that very day hostilities began between God and man. From the day of his creation until he sinned, Adam fellowshipped with

Does Salvation Produce Feelings?

God in the garden; but after he ate the forbidden fruit he ran and hid among the trees in the garden when he heard the voice of God calling, "Adam, where art thou?" And Adam said, "I heard thy voice in the garden, *and I was AFRAID . . .*" (Gen. 3:8-10). Warfare began that day, warfare between God and man; and the only way for such hostilities to cease is for man to exercise faith in God through the finished work of Jesus. When man does that, God gives peace: *"Therefore being justified by FAITH, we have PEACE with God through our Lord Jesus Christ"* (Rom. 5:1).

You may ask, "What about *joy* and salvation?" It is true that salvation brings "joy unspeakable and full of glory" (I Pet. 1:8). And what is the definition of *joy?* It is defined as "the emotion excited by the acquisition or expectation of good; gladness; delight; state of happiness; bliss."

I would be the first to agree that when a sinner exercises faith in the shed blood and finished work of Jesus and the burden of sin is lifted from the soul of that sinner, certainly his heart is filled with joy because he has *rest* and *peace with God.* But I warn you—never try to tell a sinner in the language of man how "joy" feels, because the Bible clearly declares that the joy salvation brings is "joy *unspeakable,*" and God forbid that I should try to put into words what God declares unspeakable! We are all saved in the same way. God does not save the drunkard one way and the moral man or woman in another way. We are saved by God's grace through faith in the shed blood of Jesus; but we do not all respond emotionally in the same way. We are not all of the same emotional pattern, but all who believe on Jesus for salvation receive peace, rest, and joy.

Babes In Christ

To become a Christian one must be born again, and God does the "borning." The incorruptible seed, the Word of God, brings the birth, new life in Christ.

When a person is saved, born again, he becomes a "babe in Christ," and as newborn physical babies must be fed and nourished in order to grow, so must the babe in Christ be fed and nourished in order to grow *spiritually*. I Peter 2:2 prescribes the diet for newborn Christians:

"As newborn babes, desire the sincere *milk of the Word*, that ye may grow thereby."

We can draw another illustrative comparison here between the physical and the spiritual: Just as physical babies do not all act the same way, neither do babes in Christ all act the same way. Some babies smile more than others, some cry more than others. Some stand alone and walk much sooner than others. So it is with babes in Christ. Some people, when they become children of God, weep for joy. Others laugh. Some clap their hands. But it is equally true that still others are born into the family of God without displaying any outward emotion whatsoever.

Over the years of my ministry I have seen drunkards, murderers, harlots, thieves, blasphemers, and yes—church members and outstanding civic leaders—born into the kingdom of God. I have seen some of them weep. Others smiled, others clapped their hands for joy, while some stood with no display of emotion as they received the truth and were set free from the penalty of sin, the fear of death, their hearts flooded with the peace and joy that come with salvation. Some people are more emotional than others by nature, therefore when they are saved they will *display* more emotion than others. It is a terrible mistake for personal workers and counselors to tell a seeking soul that there is a set pattern by which they should respond to the call of salvation.

I fear there will be souls in hell because Christians—including pastors—dealt with them by giving their own experience when *they* were saved, instead of giving the sinner the Word of God. They tell the sinner what kind of experience *they* had and how they "felt" when they were saved, instead of telling him *what Jesus did* to save sinners. It is the Word of God, the incorruptible seed, that brings light, faith, and life. Therefore it is the Word of God that should be given to the sinner. It is a wonderful thing to testify to what Christ has done for you, but when you are dealing with sinners who need Him, tell them from the Word of God what He *has* done—and *will do—for them!*

I know in my own heart that I am saved. I have peace with God and joy of salvation in my heart—but I am not a "shouting" Christian. If you are, God bless you! but do not try to put everyone else in your mold. We should not demand that all Christians shout, or weep, or laugh, or display whatever emotion we ourselves feel or display because of our salvation. If we do this, we will stand before God with bloody hands, and souls will burn in hell because we lifted up ourselves instead of lifting up the Lord Jesus Christ to a lost world. In John 12:32 He declared, *"I, if I be lifted up* from the earth, will draw all men unto me."

If my salvation depended on "feelings" there would be days when I would be happily saved—and other days when I would be hopelessly lost! In other words, there are days when all goes well and life is "sunny side up." But there are other days when difficulties, persecutions, illness, and many other things beset me; and if it were not that my faith is founded and secured in the Word of God, life would be worth little or nothing. So we cannot measure or weigh salvation by *"feelings."* Feelings fluctuate, but "Thus saith the Lord" is the same throughout eternity. Circumstances govern feelings, but Christ is the same yesterday, today, and forever (Heb. 13:8).

There are two extremes in religion today. One group puts entirely *too much* emphasis on emotion, while the other group has completely *outlawed* emotion in favor of card-signing, hand-shaking, formal religion. The first group sings, claps their hands, and shouts for joy—and if they do not do this they feel that they have not worshipped God or honored Him sufficiently. The second group holds services, passes out programs, and goes through forms, conducting every meeting by rules and regulations. Then when the clock says it is time for the benediction, the benediction is pronounced and the congregation goes home.

But thank God, between these two extremes there are churches where the Word of God is believed from Genesis through Revelation—and taught accordingly. In such churches, services are sometimes a bit emotional, sometimes not; and neither instance determines whether or not God has been glorified and honored. "God is a Spirit: and they that worship Him must worship Him in spirit and in truth" (John 4:24). This is what brings honor and glory to God, not emotionalism or formalism, as such.

Some Bible Conversions

The best commentary on the Bible is the Bible itself, and the best method of Bible study is to compare Scripture with Scripture, spiritual things with spiritual. Time and space will not allow us

133

to discuss all of the conversions recorded in the Scriptures, but we will look at some of the outstanding accounts, comparing them one with another.

The first convert in Europe:—

"A certain woman named Lydia, a seller of purple, of the city of Thyatira, which worshipped God, heard us: whose heart the Lord opened, that she attended unto the things which were spoken of Paul. And when she was baptized, and her household, she besought us, saying, If ye have judged me to be faithful to the Lord, come into my house, and abide there. And she constrained us" (Acts 16:14, 15).

Paul and Silas had arrived at Philippi on their missionary journey, and they had gone out to speak to a women's Bible class which met just outside the city "by a river side" (Acts 16:13). Lydia was very probably an outstanding person. She was a merchant, a seller of purple—which indicates that she was patronized by royalty, since only royalty and extremely wealthy people could afford "purple and fine linen." We are told that Lydia "worshipped God," indicating that she walked in all the light she had. But as Paul and Silas addressed the group of women, the Lord opened Lydia's heart and she believed the message the missionaries preached. Faith comes by hearing, and hearing by the Word of God. Paul certainly preached *the Word.* So Lydia believed, was converted, baptized along with her entire household, and then she invited Paul and his company to be guests in her home.

We read of nothing spectacular here insofar as Lydia's actions were concerned. Hers was a very quiet conversion. She heard the Word, she believed, she was baptized, and she opened her home to these men who were preaching the Gospel. Thus, with the conversion of this quiet, genteel "seller of purple," the Church in Europe began.

A fortuneteller saved:—

"And it came to pass, as we went to prayer, a certain damsel possessed with a spirit of divination met us, which brought her masters much gain by soothsaying. The same followed Paul and us, and cried, saying, These men are the servants of the most high God, which shew unto us the way of salvation. And this did she many days. But Paul, being grieved, turned and said to the spirit, I command thee in the name of Jesus Christ to come out of her. And he came out the same hour" (Acts 16:16-18).

We are not told that the young fortuneteller shouted *when* she was converted, nor even *afterward;* but for "many days" previous to her conversion she followed the missionaries, noisily pointing out that they were servants of the most high God and that they were showing people the way of salvation. Then when Paul cast out the demon that possessed her, she became calm, filled with rest, peace, and joy. In this instance it was Paul and Silas who got the "feeling," for when the men who had used the fortuneteller to make money for them discovered that their chance of further gain had ended with her conversion, they had Paul and Silas arrested, dragged into the market-place, and beaten unmercifully!

But as often happens in the life of the surrendered Christian, what seemed ill for the apostles turned out to the glory of God and led to another Bible conversion.

The Philippian jailer saved:—

"And when they had laid many stripes upon them, they cast them into prison, charging the jailor to keep them safely: who, having received such a charge, thrust them into the inner prison, and made their feet fast in the stocks. And at midnight Paul and Silas prayed, and sang praises unto God: and the prisoners heard them. And suddenly there was a great earthquake, so that the foundations of the prison were shaken: and immediately all the doors were opened, and every one's bands were loosed. And the keeper of the prison awaking out of his sleep, and seeing the prison doors open, he drew out his sword, and would have killed himself, supposing that the prisoners had been fled. But Paul cried with a loud voice, saying, Do thyself no harm: for we are all here.

"Then he called for a light, and sprang in, and came trembling, and fell down before Paul and Silas, and brought them out, and said, Sirs, what must I do to be saved? And they said, Believe on the Lord Jesus Christ, and thou shalt be saved, and thy house. And they spake unto him the Word of the Lord, and to all that were in his house. And he took them the same hour of the night, and washed their stripes; and was baptized, he and all his, straightway. And when he had brought them into his house, he set meat before them, and rejoiced, believing in God with all his house" (Acts 16:23-34).

Cold and hungry, backs bloody from the merciless beating they had endured, Paul and Silas were imprisoned—not simply incarcerated behind bars, but locked in the security dungeon and their feet made fast in the stocks. Hopeless? Not to these men. Instead of worrying about what might be their lot the next morning, and instead of acknowledging defeat, they prayed and sang praises to God. At the midnight hour, as they sang and praised God where all the other prisoners could hear them, God answered with an earthquake that shook the prison to its foundations. All the doors were opened and the chains loosed from all the prisoners as God acknowledged His servants who had been so cruelly mistreated and thrown in jail.

The jailer wakened from sleep, his heart struck through with fear. If the prison doors were open and the prisoners released, they had certainly fled; and if that be true, then he would pay forfeit with his own life for letting them escape! Rather than face such an ordeal he drew his sword and was about to take his own life when he heard Paul cry out through the darkness, "Do thyself no harm! We are all here!"

The jailer then called for a light, and springing in where the missionaries were, he fell down before them and cried out, "Sirs, what must I do to be saved?" They replied by giving him the only condition for salvation: *"BELIEVE on the Lord Jesus Christ, and thou shalt be saved, and thy house. And they spake unto him THE WORD OF THE LORD, and to all that were in his house."*

"Faith cometh by hearing, and hearing by the Word of God" (Rom. 10:17). But here was a man who had not *heard* the Word of God. Therefore Paul and Silas explained that salvation comes through faith in the finished work of Jesus—and then "spoke unto him the Word of the Lord" that he might hear, believe, and call on the name of Jesus. He believed, he and his household, and they were all baptized *"and rejoiced,* believing in God."

We are not told *how* this man *"rejoiced."* Did he laugh? Did he weep for joy? Did he clap his hands? The Scripture does not say. But we do know that for him all things were made new. That is, whereas the night before, he had cast his prisoners into the dungeon and locked them in the stocks without seemingly so much as a thought for their discomfort or their suffering from the beating they had received, he now took them into his own home, "washed their stripes" and "set meat before them." Saved to serve! Perhaps his rejoicing took the form of ministering to God's servants as guests in his house. At any rate, there was "joy unspeakable" in that household as the jailer "believed in God with all his house."

Blind Bartimaeus saved:—

"And they came to Jericho: and as He went out of Jericho with His disciples and a great number of people, blind Bartimaeus, the son of Timaeus, sat by the highway side begging. And when he heard that it was Jesus of Nazareth, he began to cry out, and say, Jesus, thou son of David, have mercy on me!

"And many charged him that he should hold his peace: but he cried the more a great deal, Thou son of David, have mercy on me! And Jesus stood still, and commanded him to be called. And they call the blind man, saying unto him, Be of good comfort, rise; He calleth thee. And he, casting away his garment, rose, and came to Jesus.

"And Jesus answered and said unto him, What

wilt thou that I should do unto thee? The blind man said unto Him, Lord, that I might receive my sight. And Jesus said unto him, Go thy way. Thy faith hath made thee whole. And immediately he received his sight, and followed Jesus in the way" (Mark 10:46-52).

These verses tell the complete story of how Bartimaeus received both physical and spiritual sight. We note that Jesus did not touch this man, He did not pray for him, He did nothing spectacular insofar as the crowd around Him could see. He simply "stood still," and commanded that the blind man be called. Bartimaeus immediately obeyed. He rose *and came to Jesus.* Then Jesus asked him, "What wilt thou that I should do unto thee?" and the man asked that he might receive his sight. Jesus asked him no further questions, He told him nothing to do. He said to him, "Go thy way—*thy FAITH hath made thee whole.*"

Faith comes by hearing, and hearing by the Word. Bartimaeus *believed* what Jesus said, but if he laughed, wept, clapped his hands or shouted, we are not told of it! Certainly he had a perfect right to rejoice long and noisily, but if he did so, the Holy Spirit did not think it important enough to record it. What the Word of God emphasizes here is that *faith* was exercised. This man believed what Jesus said, he did what Jesus told him to do, and he did it without hesitation or reservation.

He was saved, he received physical sight and spiritual sight, and he followed Jesus—*by FAITH, not by "feelings."*

The dying thief saved:—

"And one of the malefactors which were hanged railed on Him, saying, If thou be Christ, save thyself and us. But the other answering rebuked him, saying, Dost not thou fear God, seeing thou art in the same condemnation? And we indeed justly; for we receive the due reward of our deeds: but this Man hath done nothing amiss. And he said unto Jesus, Lord, remember me when thou comest into thy kingdom. And Jesus said unto him, Verily I say unto thee, To day shalt thou be with me in Paradise" (Luke 23:39-43).

Matthew 27:44 tells us that at first, both of the thieves who were crucified with Jesus railed on Him, along with the multitudes who passed by; but from Luke's account we know that one of the thieves changed his attitude, and the only reason for such a change was that he heard the words of Jesus. Whatever Jesus said—whether from the cross, on the Jericho road, or written in the dirt on the temple floor—was the Word of God. He spoke seven times from the cross. Faith comes by hearing, and hearing by the Word. So the thief heard—*and believed*—what Jesus said. Therefore he said, "Lord, remember me when thou comest into thy kingdom." And Jesus replied, "To day

141

shalt thou be with me in Paradise!''

Now I ask you—what kind of "feelings" did this *thief* have? He was nailed to a Roman cross, bleeding, suffering untold agony. Yet in his agony he recognized the Saviour of the world and cried out for salvation. He was saved by God's grace, grace that became his through faith. If there was any display of emotion or "feeling" it is certainly not recorded in Scripture and therefore is not important. The important part of the record is that the thief recognized his lost condition, recognized the sinless Son of God on the cross, asked to be remembered, and Jesus granted his request. I expect to meet that thief in the glorious resurrection morning—and beloved, if *you* do not meet *that* thief, then you will meet the other thief who was crucified with Jesus! the one who refused to hear the words of Jesus and did not ask to be remembered. He could have been saved as surely as the penitent thief was saved, but he did not exercise faith in the Lamb of God, dying on the cross, shedding His precious blood for the remission of sin.

The first apostolic miracle:—

"Now Peter and John went up together into the temple at the hour of prayer, being the ninth hour. And a certain man lame from his mother's womb was carried, whom they laid daily at the gate of the temple which is called Beautiful, to ask alms of them that entered into the temple; who seeing Peter and John about to go into the temple asked an alms. And Peter, fastening his eyes upon him with John, said, Look on us. And he gave heed unto them, expecting to receive something of them.

"Then Peter said, Silver and gold have I none; but such as I have give I thee: *In the name of Jesus Christ of Nazareth rise up and walk!* And he took him by the right hand, and lifted him up: and immediately his feet and ankle bones received strength. And he leaping up stood, and walked, and entered with them into the temple, walking, and leaping, and praising God. And all the people saw him walking and praising God: and they knew that it was he which sat for alms at the Beautiful gate of the temple: and they were filled with wonder and amazement at that which had happened unto him.

"And as the lame man which was healed held Peter and John, all the people ran together unto them in the porch that is called Solomon's, greatly wondering. And when Peter saw it, he answered unto the people, Ye men of Israel, why marvel ye at this? Or why look ye so earnestly on us, as though by our own power or holiness we had made this man to walk? The God of Abraham, and of Isaac, and of Jacob, the God of our fathers, hath glorified His Son Jesus; whom ye delivered up, and denied Him in the presence of Pilate, when he was determined to let Him go. But ye denied the Holy One and the Just, and desired a murderer to be granted unto you; and killed the Prince of life, whom God hath raised from the dead; whereof we are witnesses. *And His name through faith in His name hath made this man strong,* whom ye see and know: *yea, the FAITH which is by HIM hath given him this perfect soundness* in the presence of you all" (Acts 3:1-16).

We have here the account of the first apostolic miracle and the display of quite a bit of emotion which was all to the glory of God and for a definite purpose. If you will study the rest of the book of Acts you will not find another account of such a display of emotion because of the conversion of a sinner or the preaching of the apostles. It is true that on other occasions individuals were saved, such as in the house of Cornelius (Acts chapter 10). Some spoke with other tongues and glorified God. But in this particular case when the man was healed he leaped, walked, and went into the temple praising God.

His actions caused quite a stir among the people. They knew him, they were accustomed to seeing him day after day sitting by the Beautiful gate and asking alms of all who passed by. There was no denying the fact of the miracle. Then as the man put his arms around Peter and John, the people rushed up and gazed at the apostles as though they were gods.

Does Salvation Produce Feelings?

But Peter made it very clear that it was by no power invested in either himself or John that the lame man had been healed. It was *BY FAITH in the name of Jesus of Nazareth.* And what was it that gave this man his faith? *Peter told him about Jesus!* "In the name of Jesus Christ of Nazareth, rise up and walk." He believed in the name of Jesus, and when Peter took him by the hand he immediately received strength in his feet and ankles, and he walked, and leaped, and praised God.

However, in the very next chapter we are told that many heard the Word and believed, "and the number of the men was about five thousand" (Acts 4:4)—but if any of them ran, leaped, or audibly praised God it was not important enough to be included in the account.

Why this contrast? God had a reason. The man who was healed at the Beautiful gate was a man well known in that locality. Everyone knew that he had been lame since birth. Therefore, when they saw him leaping and running they could not deny that a great miracle had been performed. God gave the miracle, and He put within that man's heart the desire to run and leap and praise Him in order to witness to the Jews that the Christ preached by Peter and John was truly the Messiah promised in the Old Testament. And in Acts 4:21, 22 we read that Peter and John were threatened and forbidden to preach in the name of Jesus because *"all men glorified God for that which was done.* For the man was above forty years old, on whom this miracle of healing was shewed."

In our study, comparing Scripture with Scripture, we have seen that some Bible conversions have been very quiet and unspectacular, while in others there has been a display of emotion. Therefore, to preach that one will not display emotion when he is saved would be wrong; and by the same token it would be equally wrong to preach that everyone who is saved must display some sign of emotion. God's Word teaches neither of these things as a set rule. There is only *ONE WAY to be saved*—that is by receiving Jesus, the Gift of God. But not every born again person behaves in the same manner upon *receiving* that Gift, and according to the Word of God those who display no emotion at all are just as perfectly saved as those who behave emotionally.

The important thing is not *"Do you FEEL saved?"* It is not *"Did you WEEP when you were saved—or did you LAUGH when you were saved?"* The all-important question is "Did you put your *faith and trust* in the shed blood and finished work *of JESUS?* Did you receive Him *by faith?"* If not, then you are not saved, it matters not how much you may weep, or how much you may laugh, leap, or clap your hands.

I cannot repeat too often nor emphasize too

strongly that there is only one salvation, one way to heaven. Jesus is the way, the truth, the life (John 14:6). No man comes to the Father but by Him. "Neither is there salvation in any other: for there is none other name under heaven given among men, whereby we must be saved" (Acts 4:12). Apart from His name there is no salvation. Grace saves, and grace is God's unmerited, unearned favor. God's grace becomes ours by faith, and without faith it is impossible to please God (Heb. 11:6), and *whatsoever is NOT of faith is sin* (Rom. 14:23).

Peace with God is the gift of God—"Peace I leave with thee, my peace I give unto thee" (John 14:27).

"Therefore being justified by faith, we have peace with God" (Rom. 5:1).

Salvation is God's gift and the only way to come into possession of a gift is to receive it from the giver. The only way to be saved is to receive the Gift of God, the Lord Jesus, by faith. And if you sincerely in your heart did receive the Lord Jesus Christ as your personal Saviour, you are saved regardless of whether or not you have any emotional stir. It is not by "feelings," laughing, crying, walking, leaping, baptism, church membership, good works, giving, going, living, doing, abstaining—no. It is by grace, through faith, the gift of God, not of works (Eph. 2:8, 9).

Newly born into the family of God, we are babes

in Christ—but we are not to *remain* babes. We are to grow. And as we feed upon the Word of God we become stronger. We get more out of our Christian life because we are then more capable of understanding the things of God and doing His work. The more we put into our Christian living, the more we get out of it.

Many Christians become discouraged because they do not have the joy that some other Christians seem to have. They know someone in their church who shouts every time the congregation meets for worship, and *they themselves* want to shout. It is sad indeed when older Christians display emotions which cause younger believers to become discouraged because they cannot display the same joy as those who shout, or weep, or clap their hands, or whatever the manner in which they express their feelings. All that we do should be done to the glory of God, not that men may look upon us and say that we are "spiritual." Certainly what we do should be done in sincerity, not for the purpose of putting on a "religious show." We need to serve God with singleness of heart, spirit, and mind, that whether we eat, drink, or whatsoever we do may be done to the glory of God (I Cor. 10:31).

There are believers who actually hinder young Christians by appearing to be happy all the time. But we only see these people on Sunday and perhaps at Wednesday night prayermeeting. If we could see them through the week—on the job, or at a sink full of dirty dishes, or beside the highway standing beside their automobile which has a flat tire or refuses to start, we might see them less jubilant! There is a possibility of hindering babes in Christ if we are over-emotional and display joy which actually does not exist in the heart.

As we grow in grace and in the knowledge of our Lord and Saviour Jesus Christ, as we witness for Him and win souls, we become happier Christians and get more out of our Christian experience. But "feelings" and salvation have nothing in common. That is, salvation does not depend on feelings. Salvation does not necessarily cause one to display outward emotion. Salvation brings rest, peace, joy, tranquility, quietness, assurance. It delivers from fear. But all of these can be ours without an outward display of emotion.

Words That Bring Strength

Let me give you some Scriptures that will strengthen and comfort you and bring assurance that no display of emotion could ever bring:

". . . Have faith in God" (Mark 11:22).

". . . I have learned, in whatsoever state I am, therewith to be content. I know both how to be abased, and I know how to abound: every where and in all things I am instructed both to be full and to be hungry, both to abound and to suffer need. I can do all things through Christ which strengtheneth me" (Phil. 4:11-13).

"My God shall supply all your need according to His riches in glory by Christ Jesus" (Phil. 4:19).

"For in (Christ) dwelleth all the fulness of the Godhead bodily. And ye are complete in Him, which is the head of all principality and power" (Col. 2:9, 10).

"If ye then be risen with Christ, seek those things which are above, where Christ sitteth on the right hand of God. Set your affection on things above, not on things on the earth. For ye are dead, and your life is hid with Christ in God. When Christ, who is our life, shall appear, then shall ye also appear with Him in glory" (Col. 3:1-4).

". . . I KNOW WHOM I HAVE BELIEVED, and am persuaded that He is able to keep that which I have committed unto Him against that day" (II Tim. 1:12).

Do you remember a time—not necessarily a date, but an experience—when you were convicted of sin, realized your need of a Saviour, and received Jesus as your Saviour by faith? Do you love Jesus? If you do, these words are yours:

"We know that all things work together for good to them that love God, to them who are the called according to His purpose. . . . What shall we then say to these things? If God be for us, who can be against us? He that spared not His own Son, but delivered Him up for us all, how shall He not with Him also freely give us all things?

"Who shall lay anything to the charge of God's elect? It is God that justifieth. Who is he that condemneth? It is Christ that died, yea rather, that is risen again, who is even at the right hand of God, who also maketh intercession for us.

"Who shall separate us from the love of Christ? Shall tribulation, or distress, or persecution, or famine, or nakedness, or peril, or sword? As it is written, For thy sake we are killed all the day long; we are accounted as sheep for the slaughter.

"Nay, in all these things we are more than conquerors through Him that loved us. For I am persuaded, that neither death, nor life, nor angels, nor principalities, nor powers, nor things present, nor things to come, nor height, nor depth, nor any other creature, shall be able to separate us from the love of God, which is in Christ Jesus our Lord" (Rom. 8:28, 31-39).

Does salvation produce feelings? Salvation is Christ in your heart by faith, the Prince of Peace. Salvation produces peace, rest, freedom from fear, doubt, and worry. Salvation brings assurance because we know Jesus, and He is our salvation.

Beloved, if Jesus abides in your heart by faith, you will not spend eternity in hell. You may not shout, you may not weep, you may not laugh, you may not run and leap for joy, you may not display any outward emotion at all; but if Jesus abides in your heart you will live in heaven forever.

If you know that you are *not* saved, I urge you to bow your head and believe on the Lord Jesus Christ as your Saviour. Confess your sins and ask Him to forgive your sins and come into your heart.

According to Romans 10:9, 10 "if thou shalt confess with thy mouth the Lord Jesus, and shalt believe in thine heart that God hath raised Him from the dead, *thou shalt be saved.* For with the heart man believeth unto righteousness; and with the mouth confession is made unto salvation."

BIBLE MATHEMATICS

Bible Mathematics

"But Peter, standing up with the eleven, lifted up his voice, and said unto them, Ye men of Judaea, and all ye that dwell at Jerusalem, be this known unto you, and hearken to my words:

"For these are not drunken, as ye suppose, seeing it is but the third hour of the day. But this is that which was spoken by the prophet Joel; and it shall come to pass in the last days, saith God, I will pour out of my Spirit upon all flesh, and your sons and your daughters shall prophesy, and your young men shall see visions, and your old men shall dream dreams: and on my servants and on my handmaidens I will pour out in those days of my Spirit; and they shall prophesy: and I will shew wonders in heaven above, and signs in the earth beneath; blood, and fire, and vapour of smoke: The sun shall be turned into darkness, and the moon into blood, before that great and notable day of the Lord come: and it shall come to pass, that whosoever shall call on the name of the Lord shall be saved.

"Ye men of Israel, hear these words: Jesus of Nazareth, a Man approved of God among you by miracles and wonders and signs, which God did by Him in the midst of you, as ye yourselves also know: Him, being delivered by the determinate counsel and foreknowledge of God, ye have taken, and by wicked hands have crucified and slain: whom God hath raised up, having loosed the pains of death: because it was not possible that He should be holden of it. For David speaketh concerning Him, I foresaw the Lord always before my face, for He is on my right hand, that I should not be moved: Therefore did my heart rejoice, and my tongue was glad; moreover also my flesh shall rest in hope: because thou wilt not leave my soul in hell, neither wilt thou suffer thine Holy One to see corruption. Thou hast made known to me the ways of life; thou shalt make me full of joy with thy countenance.

"Men and brethren, let me freely speak unto you of the patriarch David, that he is both dead and buried, and his sepulchre is with us unto this day. Therefore being a prophet, and knowing that God had sworn with an oath to him, that of the fruit of his loins, according to the flesh, He would raise up Christ to sit on his throne; he seeing this before spake of the resurrection of Christ, that His soul was not left in hell, neither His flesh did see corruption.

"This Jesus hath God raised up, whereof we all are witnesses. Therefore being by the right hand of God exalted, and having received of the

Father the promise of the Holy Ghost, He hath shed forth this, which ye now see and hear. For David is not ascended into the heavens: but he saith himself, The Lord said unto my Lord, Sit thou on my right hand, until I make thy foes thy footstool. Therefore let all the house of Israel know assuredly, that God hath made that same Jesus, whom ye have crucified, both Lord and Christ.

"Now when they heard this, they were pricked in their heart, and said unto Peter and to the rest of the apostles, Men and brethren, what shall we do? Then Peter said unto them, Repent, and be baptized every one of you in the name of Jesus Christ for the remission of sins, and ye shall receive the gift of the Holy Ghost. For the promise is unto you, and to your children, and to all that are afar off, even as many as the Lord our God shall call. And with many other words did he testify and exhort, saying, Save yourselves from this untoward generation.

"Then they that gladly received his word were baptized: and the same day there were ADDED UNTO THEM about three thousand souls. And they continued stedfastly in the apostles' doctrine and fellowship, and in breaking of bread, and in prayers. And fear came upon every soul: and many wonders and signs were done by the apostles.

"And all that believed were together, and had

all things common; and sold their possessions and goods, and parted them to all men, as every man had need. And they, continuing daily with one accord in the temple, and breaking bread from house to house, did eat their meat with gladness and singleness of heart, *praising God, and having favour with all the people. AND THE LORD ADDED TO THE CHURCH DAILY SUCH AS SHOULD BE SAVED"* (Acts 2:14—47).

"Simon Peter, a servant and an apostle of Jesus Christ, to them that have obtained like precious faith with us through the righteousness of God and our Saviour Jesus Christ: Grace and peace be multiplied unto you through the knowledge of God, and of Jesus our Lord, according as His divine power hath given unto us all things that pertain unto life and godliness, through the knowledge of Him that hath called us to glory and virtue: whereby are given unto us exceeding great and precious promises: that by these ye might be partakers of the divine nature, having escaped the corruption that is in the world through lust.

"And beside this, giving all diligence, ADD TO YOUR FAITH virtue; and to virtue knowledge; and to knowledge temperance; and to temperance patience; and to patience godliness; and to godliness brotherly kindness; and to brotherly kindness charity. For if these things be in you, and abound, they make you that ye shall neither

be barren nor unfruitful in the knowledge of our
Lord Jesus Christ. But he that lacketh these
things is blind, and cannot see afar off, and hath
forgotten that he was purged from his old sins.

"Wherefore the rather, brethren, give diligence
to make your calling and election sure: for if
ye do these things, ye shall never fall: For so
an entrance shall be ministered unto you abundantly into the everlasting kingdom of our Lord
and Saviour Jesus Christ. Wherefore I will not
be negligent to put you always in remembrance
of these things, though ye know them, and be
established in the present truth. Yea, I think
it meet, as long as I am in this tabernacle, to
stir you up by putting you in remembrance; knowing that shortly I must put off this my tabernacle, even as our Lord Jesus Christ hath shewed
me" (II Pet. 1:1—14).

The Church was born on the Day of Pentecost
when, as Jesus had commanded in Luke 24:49,
one hundred and twenty believers waited in the
upper room until the Day of Pentecost was fully
come and God's promise was fulfilled in accord-
ance with Joel 2:28—32. Through the miracle of
the coming of the Holy Ghost these one hundred
and twenty persons were ADDED to the *Head
of the Church*—the Lord Jesus Christ, who is
"the Head of the Church and the Saviour of the
body" (Eph. 5:23).

The days that followed Pentecost were days of

continued ADDITION to the Church as the apostles preached and hearers believed:

"Then they that gladly received (the WORD) were baptized: and the same day there were ADDED unto them about three thousand souls . . . praising God and having favour with all the people. And the Lord ADDED to the Church daily . . . And believers were the more ADDED to the Lord, multitudes both of men and women" (Acts 2:41, 47; 5:14). Then in Acts 11:24 we read that Barnabas "was a good man, and full of the Holy Ghost and of faith: *and much people was ADDED unto the Lord.*"

In our lessons in arithmetic, as children we learned that $1+1=2$, $2+2=4$, and so on. Then as we continued our study, in the process of time we learned to (1) ADD, (2) SUBTRACT, (3) MULTIPLY, and (4) DIVIDE.

The spiritual life corresponds to the natural life in many, many ways. As Jesus walked and talked among men He set forth many deep spiritual truths by using illustrations having to do with natural life. In His Sermon on the Mount as well as *throughout* the Gospels we find His parables and illustrations. For example:

We enter physical life through the natural *birth.*

We enter spiritual life—everlasting life—through the *spiritual* birth (John 3:1–7).

We are born *physically* through life-giving *seed:* God said to Abraham, "I will make thee exceeding fruitful, and I will make nations of thee, and kings shall come out of thee. And I will establish my covenant between me and thee and thy SEED after thee in their generations for an everlasting covenant, to be a God unto thee, and to thy SEED after thee. And I will give unto thee, and to thy SEED after thee, the land wherein thou art a stranger, all the land of Canaan, for an everlasting possession; and I will be their God. And God said unto Abraham, Thou shalt keep my covenant therefore, thou, and thy SEED after thee in their generations. This is my covenant, which ye shall keep, between me and you and thy seed after thee . . ." (Gen. 17:6—10).

Many, many such references to life-giving seed can be found throughout the Bible, but physical life comes through *corruptible* seed, whereas *SPIRITUAL life* comes through *incorruptible* seed: ". . . being *born again*, not of corruptible seed, but of INCORRUPTIBLE, *by the Word of God*, which liveth and abideth for ever" (I Pet. 1:23).

"He came unto His own, and His own received Him not. But as many as received Him, to them gave He power to become the sons of God, even to them that believe on His name: *which were BORN*—not of blood, nor of the will of the flesh, nor of the will of man, but of *God*" (John 1:11—13).

". . . Except a man be *BORN again*, he cannot see the kingdom of God. . . . Except a man be

BORN of water and of the Spirit, he cannot enter into the kingdom of God" (John 3:3, 5).

James 1:18 declares, "Of (God's) own will *BE-GAT HE US with the Word of truth,* that we should be a kind of firstfruits of His creatures."

The *spiritual birth* is the *one IMPERATIVE* for entering heaven. Now let me give you the *key* to the spiritual birth:

FAITH (which brings the grace that saves us) comes *only by HEARING,* and *hearing comes only BY THE WORD OF GOD* (Rom. 10:17). Thus the WORD OF GOD is the INCORRUPTI-BLE SEED that brings the FAITH which performs the miracle of the NEW BIRTH. Jesus said, "Verily, verily, I say unto you, *He that heareth MY WORD, and believeth on Him that sent me, hath everlasting life, and shall not come into condemnation; but is passed from death unto life"* (John 5:24).

Jesus also said, "It is the Spirit that quickeneth; the flesh profiteth nothing: *the WORDS that I speak unto you, they are spirit, and they are LIFE"* (John 6:63).

Salvation Begins With ADDITION

"*. . . And the Lord ADDED to the Church daily such as should be* (were being) *saved"* (Acts 2:47).

Saved persons are added to the Church by *the Lord,* not by a church clerk. Saved persons have eternal life because *(and ONLY because)* Christ is in their hearts. But what does this have to do with ADDITION? What part does ADDITION play in salvation? The answer is: *BY FAITH we ADD CHRIST to our lives.* It was *by HEARING* that we learned the *facts* of arithmetic—i. e., our teacher (or perhaps our parents before we reached school age) told us that $1+1=2$—and we *believed* it. By *faith* we accepted it as FACT.

The same is true in the spiritual life—*we learn by HEARING*, and hearing comes by the Word of God (Rom. 10:17). The Word of God tells us that *"ALL have sinned"* (Rom. 3:23), therefore mankind deserves to spend eternity in hell. The Word then tells us, *"BUT GOD, who is rich in MERCY, for His GREAT LOVE wherewith He loved us, even when we were dead in sins, hath quickened us* (made us alive from the deadness of sin) *together with Christ; BY GRACE YE ARE SAVED"* (Eph. 2:4, 5).

Then, hearing of God's mercy, His great love and saving grace, and wanting to be saved from damnation, we receive (ADD) Jesus to our hearts by faith. He came into the world to seek and to save the lost, to give His life a ransom for many (Luke 19:10; Matt. 20:28). It is not His will that one person should perish, but that ALL should come to repentance (II Pet. 3:9). Therefore:

163

"As MANY as RECEIVED Him, to them gave He POWER to become the sons of God, even to them that believe on His name: which were born . . . of God" (John 1:12, 13).

When a person believes, receives, accepts and ADDS Jesus to his life by faith, a miracle occurs: CHRIST ENTERS THE HEART IN THE PERSON OF THE HOLY SPIRIT, and *"CHRIST in YOU"* is the hope of glory (Col. 1:27). NOW:

"If ye then be risen with Christ, seek those things which are above, where Christ sitteth on the right hand of God. Set your affection on things above, not on things on the earth. *For ye are dead, and your life is HID WITH CHRIST IN GOD"* (Col. 3:1—3). For God "hath raised us up together, and made us *sit together IN HEAVENLY PLACES IN CHRIST JESUS:* That in the ages to come He might shew the exceeding riches of His grace in His kindness toward us through Christ Jesus" (Eph. 2:6, 7).

So you see, when we ADD Christ to our lives by faith, He actually takes up His abode in our hearts. Just before His crucifixion Jesus said to His disciples, "I will pray the Father, and He shall give you another Comforter, that He may abide with you for ever; even the Spirit of truth; whom the world cannot receive, because it seeth Him not, neither knoweth Him: but ye know Him; for He dwelleth with you, and shall be in you. I will not leave you comfortless: I will come to you.   Yet a little while, and the world seeth me no more; but ye see me: because I live, ye shall live also.   At that day ye shall know that *I am in my Father, and YE in ME, and I IN YOU"* (John 14:16—20).

When Christ is ADDED to a life by faith, Christ is the ANSWER to ALL things: "What shall we then say to these things?   *If God be FOR us,* who can be *against* us? He that spared not His own Son, but delivered Him up for us all, *how shall He not with Him also freely give us ALL THINGS?"* (Rom. 8:31, 32).

IN CHRIST we are COMPLETE—and *nothing can be ADDED to completeness:* "For in Him dwelleth *all the fulness of the Godhead* bodily. And ye are *COMPLETE IN HIM, which is the HEAD of all principality and power"* (Col. 2:9, 10).

ADDING CHRIST to one's life not only brings salvation from the penalty of sin—eternal death in the lake of fire; Christ in the heart also *supplies every physical, spiritual, and eternal need:*

The Apostle Paul said, *"I can do ALL things THROUGH CHRIST which strengtheneth me. . . . But my God shall SUPPLY ALL YOUR NEED according to His riches in glory BY CHRIST JESUS"* (Phil. 4:13, 19).

The FLESH is helpless, hopeless, and destined to return to the dust from whence it came (Gen. 3:19).   Therefore the power, wisdom, and works of the flesh are worthless: "For ye see your calling, brethren, how that not many wise men after the flesh, not many mighty, not many noble, are called: But God hath chosen the foolish things of the world to confound the wise; and God hath chosen the weak things of the world to confound the things which are mighty; and base things of the world, and things which are despised, hath God chosen, yea, and things which are not, to bring to nought things that are: *That no flesh should glory in His presence. BUT OF HIM are ye in Christ Jesus, who of God is made unto us WISDOM, AND RIGHTEOUSNESS, AND SANCTIFICATION, AND REDEMPTION: That, according as it is written, He that glorieth, LET HIM GLORY IN THE LORD"* (I Cor. 1:26—31).

In His Sermon on the Mount Jesus said, *"Seek ye FIRST the kingdom of God, and His righteousness; and all these things shall be ADDED unto you"* (Matt. 6:33). "All these things" includes *every need*—food, clothes, shoes, house, car—if we *need* it, God will supply it!

Jesus rebuked His disciples for being anxious about "things." By way of illustration He used things they saw all around them every day, showing them the foolishness of anxiety about daily needs when God our heavenly Father so lovingly cares for His own, and He knows what we have need of even before we ask:

"Therefore I say unto you, Take no thought for your life, what ye shall eat, or what ye shall drink; nor yet for your body, what ye shall put on. Is not the life more than meat, and the body than raiment? *Behold the fowls of the air: for they sow not, neither do they reap, nor gather into barns; yet your heavenly Father feedeth them. ARE YE NOT MUCH BETTER THAN THEY? ...*

"And why take ye thought for raiment? Consider the lilies of the field, how they grow: They toil not, neither do they spin; and yet I say unto you, that even Solomon in all his glory was not arrayed like one of these! Wherefore, if God so clothe the grass of the field, which to day is, and to morrow is cast into the oven, shall He not much more clothe YOU, O ye of little faith? Therefore take no thought, saying, What shall we eat? or, What shall we drink? or, Wherewithal shall we be clothed? . . . for your heavenly Father KNOWETH that ye have NEED of these things" (Matt. 6:25—32).

In Matthew 10:29—31 Jesus said to His disciples, "Are not two sparrows sold for a farthing? and one of them shall not fall on the ground without your Father. But the very hairs of your head are all numbered. FEAR YE NOT THEREFORE, *YE ARE OF MORE VALUE THAN MANY SPARROWS.*"

Since Jesus takes care of the birds, since He clothes the lilies of the field in color and beauty, since He provides raiment for every stalk of grass, CAN HE NOT TAKE CARE OF HIS CHILDREN who are of much more value than any or all of these? Truly He can, and will, supply our every need according to His riches in glory!

God is never too big or too busy to care for His own. He who loved us so much that He gave His only begotten Son to die for us sees every tear that falls from our eyes: "Thou tellest my wanderings: *put thou my TEARS into thy bottle: are they not in thy book?"* (Psalm 56:8).

The Psalmist also declared, "The Lord is my Shepherd; I SHALL NOT WANT. He maketh me to lie down in green pastures: He leadeth me beside the still waters. He restoreth my soul: He leadeth me in the paths of righteousness for His name's sake. Yea, though I walk through the valley of the shadow of death, *I will fear no evil: for thou art with me;* thy rod and thy staff they comfort me. Thou preparest a table before me in the presence of mine enemies: thou anointest my head with oil; my cup runneth over. *Surely goodness and mercy shall follow me all the days of my life: AND I WILL DWELL IN THE HOUSE OF THE LORD FOR EVER"* (Psalm 23).

Beloved, if you know Christ in forgiveness of your sins, if you can truthfully say, "The Lord is my Shepherd," then you can claim *every word* in this Psalm!

As children of God we are invited to *"be careful* (anxious) *for nothing,* but *IN EVERYTHING by prayer and supplication* with thanksgiving let your requests be made known unto God" (Phil. 4:6). Certainly our God is able, because in I Corinthians 3:21—23 we read, ". . . for *ALL THINGS are your's;* whether Paul, or Apollos, or Cephas, or the world, or life, or death, or things present, or things to come; *ALL are your's; and YE ARE CHRIST'S; AND CHRIST IS GOD'S."*

II Corinthians 5:18 assures us, *"ALL things are OF GOD*, who hath reconciled us to Himself by Jesus Christ . . . ."

Therefore: Since all things are of God, and since believers are reconciled to God by Jesus Christ, "we KNOW that all things work together for good to them that love God, to them who are the called according to His purpose" (Rom. 8:28).

Since we are *sons of God NOW* (I John 3:1, 2), we have PERFECT ASSURANCE concerning our eternal home in heaven. We can say with Paul, *"I KNOW WHOM I have believed, and am persuaded that He is ABLE TO KEEP that which I have committed unto Him against that day"* (II Tim. 1:12 b).

Jesus declared, *"ALL things are possible to him that BELIEVETH"* (Mark 9:23), and when we reach the end of this pilgrim journey we will *"INHERIT all things"* (Rev. 21:7).

God has "blessed us *with all spiritual blessings* in heavenly places *IN CHRIST"* (Eph. 1:3), and we must keep in mind that whatever God gives us, whatever He does for us, and whatever He has in store for us throughout eternity is all *BECAUSE OF JESUS and for HIS sake* (Eph. 2:6,7; 4:32; I John 2:12).

Dear reader, have you ADDED JESUS to YOUR life through faith in His finished work? If you have, then you have redemption from the penalty of sin, victory over the power of sin, and—one day soon—deliverance from the very presence of sin with every need supplied, here and HEREAFTER!

If you have NOT added Jesus to your life through faith in His finished work, do it NOW:

His Word declares, "Behold, NOW is the accepted time; behold, NOW is the day of salvation" (II Cor. 6:2 b).

"Boast not thyself of to morrow; for thou knowest not what a day may bring forth" (Prov. 27:1).

"Seek ye the Lord while He may be found, call ye upon Him while He is near" (Isa. 55:6).

Jesus invites: *"Come unto ME,* all ye that labour and are heavy laden, and I will give you rest. Take my yoke upon you, and learn of me; for I am meek and lowly in heart: and ye shall find rest unto your souls. For my yoke is easy, and my burden is light" (Matt. 11:28—30).

And He promises: "All that the Father giveth me shall come to me; *and HIM THAT COMETH TO ME I WILL IN NO WISE CAST OUT"* (John 6:37).

Salvation Continues With
SUBTRACTION

Salvation *begins* with ADDITION when we ADD CHRIST to our lives by faith; but salvation is continuous in that we grow in faith, we become stronger and more fruitful as we grow in grace and in the knowledge of the Lord Jesus Christ. Then comes *subtraction,* for we are to SUBTRACT from our lives all that is not godly. God's Word commands:

"Be ye not unequally yoked together with unbelievers: for what fellowship hath righteousness with unrighteousness? and what communion hath light with darkness? And what concord hath Christ with Belial? or what part hath he that believeth with an infidel? And what agreement hath the temple of God with idols? FOR YE ARE THE TEMPLE OF THE LIVING GOD; as God hath said, I will dwell in them, and walk in them; and I will be their God, and they shall be my people. WHEREFORE COME OUT FROM AMONG THEM, AND BE YE SEPARATE, saith the Lord, AND TOUCH NOT THE UNCLEAN THING; and I will receive you, and will be a Father unto you, and ye shall be my sons and daughters, saith the Lord Almighty" (II Cor. 6: 14—18).

Then, to the Corinthian believers Paul further said, "Having therefore these promises, dearly beloved, *let us CLEANSE OURSELVES from all filthiness of the flesh and spirit,* PERFECTING HOLINESS *in the fear of God"* (II Cor. 7:1).

Some people say, "I see no harm in this, or that . . . ." The question is not "Is there *harm* in it?" but rather *"Does it GLORIFY God?"* As Christians we are to SUBTRACT from our lives anything that does not bring honor and glory to God. His Word commands it:

Paul said, *"All* things are *lawful* for me, but all things are not expedient: all things are lawful for me, but all things *edify not.* Let no man seek his own, but every man another's wealth. Whatsoever is sold in the shambles, that eat, asking no question for conscience sake: For the earth is the Lord's, and the fulness thereof. If any of them that believe not bid you to a feast, and ye be disposed to go; whatsoever is set before you, eat, asking no question for conscience sake. But if any man say unto you, This is offered in sacrifice unto idols, eat not for his sake that shewed it, and for conscience sake: for the earth is the Lord's, and the fulness thereof: Conscience, I say, not thine own, but of the other: for why is my liberty judged of another man's conscience? For if I by grace be a partaker, why am I evil spoken of for that for which I give thanks?

"WHETHER THEREFORE YE EAT, OR DRINK, OR WHATSOEVER YE DO, DO ALL TO THE GLORY OF GOD. GIVE NONE OF-FENCE, NEITHER TO THE JEWS, NOR TO

THE GENTILES, NOR TO THE CHURCH OF GOD: Even as I please all men in all things, not seeking mine own profit, but the profit of many, THAT THEY MAY BE SAVED" (I Cor. 10:23—33).

Writing to the believers in Ephesus Paul gave admonition concerning certain *persons and things which should be SUBTRACTED* from the life of the believer:

"Be ye therefore followers of God, as dear children: and walk in love, as Christ also hath loved us, and hath given Himself for us an offering and a sacrifice to God for a sweetsmelling savour. But fornication, and all uncleanness, or covetousness, let it not be once named among you, as becometh saints; neither filthiness, nor foolish talking, nor jesting, which are not convenient: but rather giving of thanks.

"For this ye know, that no whoremonger, nor unclean person, nor covetous man, who is an idolater, hath any inheritance in the kingdom of Christ and of God. Let no man deceive you with vain words: for because of these things cometh the wrath of God upon the children of disobedience. BE NOT YE THEREFORE PARTAKERS WITH THEM. For ye were sometimes darkness, but now are ye light in the Lord: walk as children of light: (For the fruit of the Spirit is in all goodness and righteousness and truth;) proving what is acceptable unto the Lord. And have NO FELLOWSHIP with the UNFRUITFUL WORKS OF DARKNESS, but rather reprove them. For it is a shame even to speak of those things which are done of them in secret. But all things that are reproved are made manifest by the light: for whatsoever doth make manifest is light.

"Wherefore He saith, Awake thou that sleepest, and arise from the dead, and Christ shall give thee light. See then that ye walk circumspectly, not as fools, but as wise, redeeming the time, because the days are evil. Wherefore be ye not unwise, but understanding what the will of the Lord is" (Eph. 5:1—17).

Writing to Titus, his son in the ministry, Paul said: "The grace of God that bringeth salvation hath appeared to all men, teaching us that, denying ungodliness and worldly lusts, we should live soberly, righteously, and godly, in this present world; looking for that blessed hope, and the glorious appearing of the great God and our Saviour Jesus Christ; who gave Himself for us, that He might redeem us from all iniquity, and purify unto Himself a peculiar people, zealous of good works" (Tit. 2:11—14).

God will do for us what we cannot do for ourselves, but He expects us to do for ourselves *simply because we ARE His children.* For example, on many occasions Christians who use tobacco have said to me, "Mr. Greene, some of my Christian friends tell me that I should give up tobacco, but I see no wrong in using it. However, if the Lord Jesus will remove my *desire* for tobacco I will *quit* using it." Certainly! If the desire were *miraculously removed* I guess they WOULD quit!

Beloved, God expects us to be strong in HIM, and in the power of His might. When the born again believer really *wants* to give up (SUBTRACT) bad habits from his life, *God will give that believer the will power and the strength to do so.* Here is the prescription for victory:

"Wherefore seeing we also are compassed about with so great a cloud of witnesses, let us lay aside every weight, and the sin which doth so easily beset us, and let us run with patience the race that is set before us, *LOOKING UNTO JESUS, THE AUTHOR AND FINISHER OF OUR FAITH; who for the joy that was set before Him endured the cross, despising the shame, and is set down at the right hand of the throne of God"* (Heb. 12:1, 2).

The place of *separation unto the Lord Jesus* is the place of *purity,* and the place of purity is the place of *power;* but if we are to have purity and power *we MUST obey* the following negative commandments of our Lord and SUBTRACT these persons and things from our lives:

GIVE not: "GIVE NOT that which is holy unto the dogs, neither cast ye your pearls before swine, lest they trample them under their feet, and turn again and rend you" (Matt. 7:6).

ENTER not: "Watch and pray, that ye *ENTER NOT into temptation:* the spirit indeed is willing, but the flesh is weak" (Matt. 26:41).

BE not: "Be ye not unequally *yoked together with UNBELIEVERS:* for what fellowship hath righteousness with unrighteousness? and what communion hath light with darkness?" (II Cor. 6:14).

TOUCH not: "Come out from among them, and be ye separate, saith the Lord, and *TOUCH NOT the unclean thing;* and I will receive you" (II Cor. 6:17).

LOVE not: "Love not *the WORLD,* neither the things that are IN the world. If any man love the world, the love of the Father is not in him. For all that is in the world, the lust of the flesh, and the lust of the eyes, and the pride of life, is not of the Father, but is of the world. And the world passeth away, and the lust thereof: but he that doeth the will of God abideth for ever" (I John 2:15—17).

WALK not: "Blessed is the man that *walketh not in the counsel of the UNGODLY,* nor standeth in the way of sinners, nor sitteth in the seat of the scornful. But his delight is in the law of the Lord; and in His law doth he meditate day and night" (Psalm 1:1, 2).

The Christian life begins with the *positive*—by ADDITION. But the Christian life grows and the light shines brighter as we apply the *negative* by SUBTRACTING the things of the world from our daily life and making room for righteousness in all we do or say.

Bible Proof of True Salvation: —

There are several passages in the New Testament which tell of different persons who proved their salvation by *giving up* (SUBTRACTING) *certain things* from their lives after they were saved:

Luke 19:1—10 tells of *Zacchaeus,* a tax collector. He was a small man, and in order to get a glimpse of Jesus as He passed by, Zacchaeus climbed up in a sycamore tree. From his position in the tree he could then see over the heads of the crowd. But "when Jesus came to the place, *He looked up, and saw him,* and said unto him, Zacchaeus, make haste, and come down; for to day I must abide at thy house." Zacchaeus quickly came down and received Jesus "joyfully."

It seems that in that day most of the tax collectors were thieves. They took exorbitant taxes from the people, gave the government the allotted amount, and kept the rest of the money for themselves. But Zacchaeus had now received Jesus, and that made a difference in his way of life. So he said, "Behold, Lord, the half of my goods I give to the poor; and if I have taken any thing from any man by false accusation, I RESTORE HIM FOURFOLD!" When this little tax collector met Jesus, *he SUBTRACTED cheating from his life;* and instead of taking from his fellowman unjustly he GAVE to the poor!

To the believers in Rome, Paul wrote: "God be thanked, that ye were the servants of sin, but ye have obeyed from the heart that form of doctrine which was delivered you." (Here is ADDITION.) "Being then made *free from sin* (SUBTRACTION), ye became the servants of righteousness" (Rom. 6:17, 18). These Romans who had been servants of sin *subtracted* themselves from sin's slavery and became bondslaves of the Lord Jesus Christ. God's Word declares that when a person becomes a child of God *OLD things pass away,* they are SUBTRACTED from the believer's life, and all things become new (II Cor. 5:17).

The Holy Spirit led Paul into the city of Ephesus, and God used him there in a very special way. Great revival broke out in the city and many were converted. They then proved their conversion by SUBTRACTING from their lives the instruments and practices of the "curious arts" which were prevalent in Ephesus at that time:

"And many that believed came, and confessed, *and shewed their deeds.* Many of them also which used curious arts brought their books together, *AND BURNED THEM BEFORE ALL MEN:* and they counted the price of them, and found it fifty thousand pieces of silver" (Acts 19:18, 19). What a bonfire that must have been—and what a testimony as these new Christians put away the old life, SUBTRACTING whatever was not unto righteousness!

Corinth was a wicked city, steeped in immorality. Paul preached the Gospel there, many were saved, and they proved their conversion by SUBTRACTING from their lives the evil course they had been following. In I Corinthians 6:9—11 Paul wrote, "Know ye not that the unrighteous shall not inherit the kingdom of God? Be not deceived: neither fornicators, nor idolaters, nor adulterers, nor effeminate, nor abusers of themselves with mankind, nor thieves, nor covetous, nor drunkards, nor revilers, nor extortioners, shall inherit the kingdom of God. AND SUCH WERE SOME OF YOU: BUT YE ARE WASHED, BUT YE ARE SANCTIFIED, BUT YE ARE JUSTIFIED in the name of the Lord Jesus, and by the Spirit of our God."

ADDITION always precedes SUBTRACTION. The idolaters of Thessalonica heard Paul's preaching of the grace of God and their lives were completely changed. Paul tells us about it in his first epistle to the church in Thessalonica:

"Our Gospel came not unto you in word only, but also in power, and in the Holy Ghost, and in much assurance; as ye know what manner of men we were among you for your sake. And ye became followers of us, and of the Lord, having received the Word in much affliction, with joy of the Holy Ghost: so that ye were ensamples to all that believe in Macedonia and Achaia. For from you sounded out the Word of the Lord not only in Macedonia and Achaia, but also in every place your faith to God-ward is spread abroad; so that we need not to speak any thing. For they themselves shew of us what manner of entering in we had unto you, and *how ye turned to God* (ADDITION) *from idols* (SUBTRACTION) *to serve the living and true God, and to wait for His Son from heaven,* whom He raised from the dead, even Jesus, which delivered us from the wrath to come" (I Thess. 1:5—10).

Jesus "gave Himself for us, that He might redeem us *from ALL INIQUITY*" (Tit. 2:14). Therefore believers, children of God, are commanded to "abstain from *all appearance of evil*" (I Thess. 5:22). We are to lay aside (SUBTRACT from our lives) "all malice, and all guile, and hypocrisies, and envies, and all evil speakings" (I Pet. 2:1). We must SUBTRACT "all bitterness, and wrath, and anger, and clamour, and evil speaking" (Eph. 4:31). We are to "put off (SUBTRACT) all these: anger, wrath, malice, blasphemy, filthy communication . . . ." and we are to deal honestly with one another. We have "put off (SUBTRACTED) the old man with his deeds; and have put on (ADDED) the new man, which is renewed in knowledge after the image of Him that created him" (Col. 3:8—10).

By obeying God's commands for our lives we prove our love for Him, our loyalty to Him, and when we are obedient to His Word He will not deny us His blessings.

MULTIPLICATION

Salvation begins with ADDITION, continues day by day as we grow in grace and in knowledge of our Lord and Saviour Jesus Christ, and as we grow we SUBTRACT from our daily living those things which do not bring glory or honor to God. Then, as we continue to feed on the milk and the meat of the Word (I Pet. 2:2) we realize that *we are also to MULTIPLY.*

We are saved to SERVE. God never saved a soul in order that that soul might sit down, fold his hands, and simply "enjoy" salvation! Surely *salvation brings JOY,* but the Christian who has "joy unspeakable and full of glory" (I Pet. 1:8) is the Christian who wins souls.

A Command As Well As A Privilege:—

Fellow Christian, it is a great and glorious privilege to win souls! God *could* have sent *angels* to be His witnesses on earth, but He gave *man* the honor of witnessing, teaching, and preaching— giving out the message of salvation. But soul-winning is not only a privilege—it is also a COM-MAND. Jesus commanded His disciples, *"GO YE, therefore, and TEACH ALL NATIONS, bap-*

tizing *them in the name of the Father, and of the Son, and of the Holy Ghost: teaching them to observe ALL THINGS whatsoever I have COM-MANDED YOU:* and, lo, I am with you alway, even unto the end of the world" (Matt. 28:19, 20).

Why did Jesus command His disciples to tarry in Jerusalem after His ascension "until ye be en-dued with power from on high"? Was it that they might become great men, miracle-workers? or that they might boast of their heavenly power? Indeed not! Acts 1:8 answers the question: "Ye shall receive power, after that the Holy Ghost is come upon you: and *YE SHALL BE WITNESSES UNTO ME both in Jerusalem, and in all Judaea, and in Samaria, and unto THE UTTERMOST PART OF THE EARTH.*"

God has never bestowed His power on anyone simply that man might boast and brag about his ability. God endues men with power in order for them to WITNESS to His saving grace, that souls may be MULTIPLIED, saved from hell, and added to the family of God. John the Bap-tist, forerunner of Jesus, could have made a great name for himself because *"Jerusalem,* and *all Judaea,* and *all the region round about Jordan"* went out to hear him, "and were baptized of him in Jordan, confessing their sins" (Matt. 3:5, 6). But John did not come into the world to make a name for *himself.* He came to *announce* a name—*THE NAME OF JESUS.* That is the

responsibility and privilege of Christians today—
to point men to Jesus. Only *through His name*
can men be saved, "neither is there salvation in
any other: for there is none other name under
heaven given among men, whereby we must be
saved" (Acts 4:12).

We see the process of MULTIPLICATION applied to Christianity even while Jesus carried on
His earthly ministry. Andrew, Simon Peter's brother, was a disciple of John the Baptist. But one
day Andrew met Jesus—and the next thing he
did was to find his brother, Simon, and tell him,
"We have found the Messias, which is, being
interpreted, the CHRIST!" And he brought Peter
to Jesus. The next day Jesus found Philip and
called him. Philip immediately found Nathanael
and brought him to Jesus. Thus did the believers
begin to MULTIPLY (John 1:40—49).

Andrew could not have realized the scope of
his bringing Peter to Jesus, but it was Peter, an
ordinary fisherman, who preached on the Day
of Pentecost when three thousand souls were saved
(Acts 2:41). From Pentecost forward, day by day,
souls were added to the Church as believers MUL-
TIPLIED:

"And they, continuing daily with one accord
in the temple, and breaking bread from house
to house, did eat their meat with gladness and
singleness of heart, praising God, and having favour with all the people. *And the Lord added*

to the Church DAILY such as (were being) saved"
(Acts 2:46, 47).

"And by the hands of the apostles were many
signs and wonders wrought among the people . . .
and believers were the more added to the Lord,
multitudes both of men and women" (Acts 5:12—
14).

"For (Barnabas) was a good man, and full
of the Holy Ghost and of faith: and much people
was added unto the Lord" (Acts 11:24).

True Believers Bear Fruit:—

Jesus said to His disciples, "I am the true
vine, and my Father is the husbandman. *Every
branch in me that beareth not fruit He taketh
away:* and *every branch that beareth FRUIT,
He purgeth it, that it may bring forth MORE
FRUIT. . . . I am the VINE, ye are the BRANCH-
ES: He that abideth in me, and I in him, the
same bringeth forth MUCH FRUIT:* for without
me ye can do nothing. . . . *Herein is my Father
glorified, that ye bear MUCH FRUIT;* so shall ye
be my disciples. . . . Ye have not chosen me, but
*I have chosen you, and ordained you, that ye
should GO AND BRING FORTH FRUIT,* and
that your FRUIT should remain: that whatsoever ye shall ask of the Father in my name, He
may give it you" (John 15:1—16 in part).

In this passage we see "fruit . . . *more* fruit . . .
MUCH fruit," and it is when we bear *MUCH*

fruit that we glorify our heavenly Father. Therefore it should be the heart's desire of every believer to bear fruit in abundance. We should strive to bear fruit in order to bring glory and honor to God who loved us so much that He gave His only begotten Son to die on the cross that we, through Him, might be saved.

Believers Are Lights In A Dark World:—

Jesus said to His disciples, *"Ye are the LIGHT of the world. . . .* Let your LIGHT so shine before men, that they may *see* your good works, and glorify your Father which is in heaven"* (Matt. 5:14, 16).

In John 9:5 Jesus declared, *"As long as I am IN the world, I am the LIGHT of the world,"* but until He comes again *His children* are lights in this dark, sinful world. The sinner will not read the Bible. He is dead in sin, he abides in darkness, he is without understanding (Eph. 2:1; II Cor. 4:3, 4; I Cor. 2:14). Therefore it is a solemn duty, as well as a glorious privilege, for those of us who know Jesus to let our light shine so that unbelievers with whom we come in contact will see and know that our *salvation is real!* "Faith without works is dead" (James 2:26). Where salvation is, where Jesus dwells in the heart in the Person of the Holy Spirit, *there will be LIGHT!* Where there is *life* there *must* be *light.* Where there is *spiritual* life there will be light.

We cannot all be beacons on a hill, but many times it is *the "lower lights"* that guide the great ships around the rocks and bring them safely to shore. It is the small, landing lights along the runway that bring the planes in for a safe and sure landing on stormy nights. The same is true in the spiritual life. So many times, lights that seem to be only "candles" for Jesus can reach men and win souls that BEACON LIGHTS (such as big preachers) could never win.

In the Person of the Holy Spirit, Jesus abides in the heart of every believer—and He shines through us! Simeon said of Jesus, *"Mine eyes have SEEN thy salvation,* which thou hast prepared before the face of ALL PEOPLE; *A LIGHT to lighten the Gentiles, and the glory of thy people Israel"* (Luke 2:30—32). When Jesus came, "the people which sat in darkness saw GREAT LIGHT; and to them which sat in the region and shadow of death, LIGHT is sprung up" (Matt. 4:16). There are multitudes who still sit in the darkness of sin and in the regions of death. If we do not show them the LIGHT, if we do not SHINE FOR JESUS, these poor, darkened souls will die in their sin and spend eternity in "the blackness of darkness forever" (Jude 13).

LIGHT warms, illuminates, gladdens, makes beautiful—and there is *healing* in its power. Therefore as children of God, lights in the world, we should be warm in our love for our fellowman, illuminating in our testimony, gladdening in our daily life, beautifying in holiness of character, healing in our service to others in the name of Jesus. Above all things we should be faithful in obedience to Him who is THE LIGHT OF OUR LIFE! Just as physical light is necessary to give life to the seed that comes forth from the earth, so the testimony of Christians is necessary that men lost in the darkness of sin may know spiritual life *through the incorruptible Seed*, the Word of God (I Pet. 1:23).

The Apostle Paul gave us an outline for God's method of *spiritual MULTIPLICATION in this Day of Grace:* In Romans 10:13 Paul declared, *"Whosoever shall call upon the name of the Lord shall be saved."* That seems so simple, easy, and ordinary—and it is! But there is more to it than just saying, "O, LORD!" Jesus makes this clear in Matthew 7:21 where He said, "Not every one that saith unto me, *Lord, Lord,* shall enter into the kingdom of heaven; *BUT HE THAT DOETH THE WILL OF MY FATHER which is in heaven."* Not all will be saved who simply say, *"Lord, Lord."* Something else must be done—not "works of righteousness," but THE WILL OF GOD.

What IS the will of God, and how does one find it? The Word of God answers: "THIS is the will of Him (God) that sent me: that every one which seeth the Son, AND BELIEVETH ON HIM, may have everlasting life . . ." (John

6:40).

But how can a poor, dead, blind sinner *see and believe on Jesus?* Again we find the answer in God's Word:

"How then shall they *CALL on Him* in whom they *have NOT BELIEVED?* And how shall they *BELIEVE in Him* of whom they *have NOT HEARD?* And *how shall they HEAR without a preacher?* And *how shall they PREACH except they be SENT?* . . . So then *FAITH COMETH BY HEARING, and hearing by THE WORD OF GOD"* (Rom. 10:14—17 in part).

The sinner cannot see, he is blinded by the god of this world, until we show him the LIGHT by our life and testimony. Thus *the believer is the PREACHER.* In Acts 8:4 we are told that the believers who were "scattered abroad *went every where PREACHING THE WORD."* The entrance of the Word gives LIGHT (Psalm 119: 130).

Believers *testify* to the saving grace of God. We let our light shine. The sinner hears the testimony and sees Jesus in our daily living. Seeing and HEARING, he believes. Believing, he CALLS. Calling signifies FAITH, and faith brings saving GRACE:

"By GRACE are ye saved through FAITH; and that not of yourselves: It is the gift of God: *not of WORKS* . . ." (Eph. 2:8, 9). We are not *saved* by works, but ALL TRUE BELIEVERS

WORK. There is no such thing as an IDLE, FRUITLESS, "WORKLESS" Christian. The following Scriptures will show you what I mean:

Christians are WORKMEN to *work* for Jesus: "A certain man had two sons; and he came to the first, and said, *Son, go WORK to day in my vineyard*" (Matt. 21:28).

Christians are LIGHTS to *shine* for Jesus: "Let your LIGHT so *shine before men,* that they may see your good works, and glorify your Father which is in heaven" (Matt. 5:16).

Christians are BRANCHES to *bear fruit* for Jesus: "Herein is my Father glorified, that ye *bear MUCH fruit;* so shall ye be my disciples" (John 15:8).

Christians are WITNESSES to *testify* for Jesus: ". . . that repentance and remission of sins should be preached in His name among all nations, beginning at Jerusalem. And *ye are witnesses of these things*" (Luke 24:47, 48).

Christians are SERVANTS to *serve* Jesus: "If I then, your Lord and Master, have washed your feet; ye also ought to wash one another's feet. For *I have given you an example,* that ye should do as I have done to you" (John 13:14, 15).

Christians are SOLDIERS to *fight* for Jesus: "Thou therefore endure hardness, as a good *soldier of Jesus Christ.* No man that warreth entangleth himself with the affairs of this life; that he may please Him who hath chosen him to be a soldier"

(II Tim. 2:3, 4).

Christians are PILGRIMS and STRANGERS in this world. Therefore we are to abstain from things of the world and *dedicate our all* to Jesus: "Dearly beloved, I beseech you as strangers and pilgrims, *abstain from fleshly lusts,* which war against the soul" (I Pet. 2:11).

Fellow Christian, have you ever won a soul to Jesus? Are you shining for Him? Have you ADDED Jesus to your life by faith and SUBTRACTED from your life those things which are not to the glory of God? Are you a loyal soldier of the cross? If you are NOT winning souls and MULTIPLYING for Jesus you had better check up on your relationship with Him and see if you are really saved.

DIVISION

Salvation begins by ADDING Christ to our lives by faith. As we grow in grace and in the knowledge of our Lord we SUBTRACT from our lives those things which do not bring glory to God and to our Lord and Saviour, Jesus Christ. We are then ready to bring forth fruit and MULTIPLY by winning souls.

And then, in the spiritual life, *DIVISION is sure to follow addition, subtraction, and multiplication!* Jesus said, "Suppose ye that I am come to give peace on earth? I tell you, Nay; but rather DIVISION: For from henceforth there

190

shall be five in one house DIVIDED, three against two, and two against three. The father shall be DIVIDED against the son, and the son against the father; the mother against the daughter, and the daughter against the mother; the mother in law against her daughter in law, and the daughter in law against her mother in law" (Luke 12:51—53).

It is true that Jesus is "the Prince of Peace" (Isa. 9:6), and He GIVES peace to individuals who believe on Him. He said to His disciples, "Peace I leave with you, MY PEACE I give unto you; not as the world giveth, give I unto you. Let not your heart be troubled, neither let it be afraid" (John 14:27). The Apostle Paul declared, *"Therefore being justified by faith, we have PEACE WITH GOD through our Lord Jesus Christ"* (Rom. 5:1). But many times the very fact that peace comes into the heart of a wife, husband, or child in a home brings about a DIVISION. The *unsaved* members of a family cannot understand the change in those who have been saved, and fellowship between them is broken.

Yes, in spite of the peace Jesus gives to the individual heart in which He dwells, He was and still IS a DIVIDER OF MEN. He divided every group before whom He spoke during His public ministry. This is clearly set forth in John 7:40—43:

"Many of the people therefore, when they heard

this saying, said, Of a truth this is the Prophet. Others said, This is the Christ. But some said, Shall Christ come out of Galilee? Hath not the Scripture said, That Christ cometh of the seed of David, and out of the town of Bethlehem, where David was? SO THERE WAS A DIVISION AMONG THE PEOPLE BECAUSE OF HIM." (Read also John 9:16 and John 10:17—19.)

After the crucifixion, burial, resurrection, and ascension of Jesus the *disciples* became *dividers of men* because they preached the same Gospel Jesus preached. In Acts 14:1—4 when Paul and Barnabas preached at Iconium, many believed—"but the unbelieving Jews stirred up the Gentiles" *until the entire city was DIVIDED*, part of the people holding with the Jews and part of them with the apostles.

Paul's preaching stirred up such dissension and DIVISION between the Pharisees and Sadducees that the Roman guard was called in to rescue the apostle from the mob, lest he be torn in pieces (Acts 23:6—10).

FACE IT, beloved—*Christianity DIVIDES men!* A Christian is a new creation in Christ Jesus. He no longer loves the things of the world, he no longer speaks the language of the world. Thus there comes A GREAT DIVISION among men. They are divided into two groups: (1) *Sons of God* (I John 3:1, 2) and (2) *Sons of the devil* (John 8:44).

Under inspiration of the Holy Spirit, Peter described believers in these words:

"Ye are a chosen generation, a royal priesthood, an holy nation, A PECULIAR PEOPLE: that ye should shew forth the praises of Him who hath called you out of darkness into His marvellous light" (I Pet. 2:9).

Some people say, "I have not become a Christian because I am afraid I could not give up the world." *Beloved, become A CHRISTIAN and the world will give YOU up!* The most miserable person on earth is an unbeliever in the company of born again Christians who are talking about Jesus and His soon coming to receive His own unto Himself. Becoming a Christian may cause you to lose what you choose to call "friends," *but I say that a person who wants you to serve the devil and spend eternity in hell is NOT your friend!* You may lose association with some of your own family—but consider this, dear reader: *If you lose YOUR SOUL you have lost ALL! "For what is a man PROFITED, if he shall GAIN THE WHOLE WORLD, and lose his own soul? . . ."* (Matt. 16:26).

The Last Great Division

There is a day coming when the great Divider of men will separate the righteous from the unrighteous forever: "When the Son of man shall come in His glory, and all the holy angels with

Him, then shall He sit upon the throne of His glory: and before Him shall be gathered all nations:
and He shall *separate them one from another, as a
shepherd DIVIDETH his sheep from the goats:*
and He shall set the sheep on His right hand, but
the goats on the left. Then shall the King say unto them on His right hand, Come, ye blessed of my
Father, inherit the kingdom prepared for you from
the foundation of the world: . . . Then shall He say
also unto them on the left hand, Depart from me,
ye cursed, into everlasting fire, prepared for the
devil and his angels: . . . And these shall go away
into everlasting punishment: but the righteous
into life eternal'' (Matt. 25:31−46 in part).

I realize that this speaks of the judgment of the
nations, and that the Great White Throne judgment will come later; but this passage declares *the
Bible fact* that *there IS a DIVIDING day coming!*
At the Great White Throne judgment *the wicked of
all ages* will be judged and forever separated from
God, from heaven, and from the righteous (Rev.
20:11−15).

In closing this message I ask you, dear reader,
ARE YOU SAVED? Have you ADDED Christ to
your life by faith? If not, salvation is for you. It
is not God's will that you perish, He wants you to
be saved—and you *can* be saved if you want to be.
Read the following verses, do what they tell you to
do, and Jesus will come into your heart. He will
save you—and you will know it. Then write me

and tell me that you have trusted Jesus, and let me rejoice with you.

"For God so loved the world, that He gave His only begotten Son, that whosoever believeth in Him should not perish, but have everlasting life. . . . He that believeth on Him is not condemned: but he that believeth not is condemned already, because he hath not believed in the name of the only begotten Son of God. . . . He that believeth on the Son hath everlasting life: and he that believeth not the Son shall not see life; but the wrath of God abideth on him" (John 3:16, 18, 36).

"Verily, verily, I say unto you, He that heareth my word, and believeth on Him that sent me, hath everlasting life, and shall not come into condemnation; but is passed from death unto life" (John 5:24).

"If thou shalt confess with thy mouth the Lord Jesus, and shalt believe in thine heart that God hath raised Him from the dead, thou shalt be saved. For with the heart man believeth unto righteousness; and with the mouth confession is made unto salvation" (Rom. 10:9, 10).

"For by grace are ye saved through faith; and that not of yourselves: it is the gift of God: Not of works, lest any man should boast" (Eph. 2: 8, 9).

"Believe on the Lord Jesus Christ, and THOU SHALT BE SAVED . . ." (Acts 16:31).